Fruit Desserts

GENERAL EDITOR
CHUCK WILLIAMS

RECIPES
LORA BRODY

PHOTOGRAPHY
ALLAN ROSENBERG

TIME
LIFE
BOOKS

Time-Life Books is a division of Time Life Inc.
Time-Life is a trademark of Time Warner Inc. U.S.A.

President and CEO: John M. Fahey, Jr.
President, Time-Life Books: John D. Hall

TIME-LIFE CUSTOM PUBLISHING

Vice President and Publisher: Terry Newell
Sales Director: Frances C. Mangan
Editorial Director: Donia Steele

WILLIAMS-SONOMA
Founder/Vice-Chairman: Chuck Williams

WELDON OWEN INC.
President: John Owen
Publisher: Wendely Harvey
Managing Editor: Laurie Wertz
Consulting Editor: Norman Kolpas
Copy Editor: Sharon Silva
Editorial Assistant: Janique Poncelet
Design: John Bull, The Book Design Company
Production: James Obata, Stephanie Sherman,
    Mick Bagnato
Food Photographer: Allan Rosenberg
Additional Food Photography: Allen V. Lott
Primary Food & Prop Stylist: Sandra Griswold
Food Stylist: Heidi Gintner
Assistant Food Stylists: Danielle Di Salvo,
    Mara Barot
Prop Assistant: Elizabeth Ruegg
Glossary Illustrations: Alice Harth

The Williams-Sonoma Kitchen Library
conceived and produced by Weldon Owen Inc.
814 Montgomery St., San Francisco, CA 94133

In collaboration with Williams-Sonoma
3250 Van Ness Ave., San Francisco, CA 94109

Production by Mandarin Offset, Hong Kong
Printed in China

A Note on Weights and Measures:
All recipes include customary U.S. and metric
measurements. Metric conversions are based on
a standard developed for these books and have
been rounded off. Actual weights may vary.

A Weldon Owen Production

Copyright © 1994 Weldon Owen Inc.
Reprinted in 1994; 1995

Library of Congress
Cataloging-in-Publication Data:

Brody, Lora, 1945-
    Fruit desserts / general editor, Chuck Williams ; recipes,
Lora Brody ; photography, Allan Rosenberg.
        p.   cm. — (Williams-Sonoma kitchen library)
    Includes index.
    ISBN 0-7835-0287-7
    1. Desserts. 2. Cookery (Fruit)   I. Williams, Chuck.
II. Title.   III. Series.
TX773.B78   1994
641.8'6—dc20   93-48182
                                        CIP

Contents

INTRODUCTION

The first fruit dessert in history could not have been simpler or had more profound an effect: an apple, handed by Eve to Adam.

Humankind has come a long way since the Garden of Eden. But if one culinary fact has remained constant, it's our fondness for fruit. Fresh, sweet and juicy, fruit makes the perfect end to a meal, particularly in these health-conscious times when *light* is arguably the most often-heard word in culinary circles.

We've been blessed with a cornucopia from which to choose: succulent peaches, plums, nectarines and pears; tangy oranges, lemons, limes and grapefruit; exotic-tasting mangoes, pineapples, bananas and kiwifruits; bright, jewellike berries; and, yes, crisp apples of every description.

This book celebrates fruit in all its dazzling variety. It begins with some lessons that emphasize how very easy fruit desserts are to make: a guide to the few basic pieces of kitchen equipment you'll need; and an overview of simple edible containers and sauces that will give your fruit desserts an extra flourish.

The two chapters that follow present 45 fruit dessert recipes, organized by the seasonality of their main ingredients. Of course, modern-day air freight makes it possible to find virtually any fruit at any time of year in a well-stocked food store. But the chapter divisions are intended to encourage you to feature on your table the finest quality, locally grown, in-season ingredients at the most reasonable prices.

Allow me to return, for a moment, to the topic of lightness—an area in which fruit reigns over all other dessert ingredients. You'll find a good selection of rich desserts in this book, to be sure. But a number of them are also exceptionally light—and you can make many of the simpler, unbaked desserts lighter still by decreasing the amounts of sugar, cream or butter.

I hope you'll give these recipes the chance to prove that enjoying a fruit dessert need not increase your waistline.

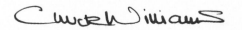

EQUIPMENT

Basic tools for making fruit desserts reflect the utter simplicity of the recipes themselves

The selection of kitchen equipment shown here will meet virtually any of the few specialized tasks detailed in this book's recipes. Part of the joy of a fruit dessert, after all, lies in its simplicity. Just as important as those tools shown, however, is a range of equipment that should be found in any kitchen.

For the inevitable cutting, slicing and chopping involved in preparing most fruits, a set of good-quality kitchen knives with sharp, stainless-steel blades securely attached to comfortable, sturdy handles will help the work go quickly and safely. Mixing bowls in a range of sizes are essential, and should include nonmetal bowls that will not react with certain acidic fruits. Good-quality saucepans, frying pans and sauté pans make stove-top cooking an efficient pleasure. And an electric mixer, a food processor and a blender take time and effort out of longer or more arduous cooking tasks.

1. Measuring Cups and Spoons
In graduated sizes, for accurate measuring of large and small quantities of dry ingredients. Straight rims allow dry ingredients to be evenly leveled. Choose stainless steel for accuracy and sturdiness.

2. Zester
Small, sharp holes at end of stainless-steel blade cut citrus zest from peels in fine shreds. Choose a model with a sturdy, well-attached handle.

3. Cherry Pitter
Hinged utensil securely grasps an individual cherry and pushes out its pit.

4. Spatulas
Small, narrow-bladed spatulas neatly spread icings or other toppings, as well as accurately level the surface of dry ingredients with the rims of measuring cups.

5. Cheesecloth
For lining coeur à la crème molds. Muslin can also be used.

6. Coeur à la Crème Molds
Individual heart-shaped 1-cup (8-fl oz/250-ml) molds for forming and for draining excess moisture from the traditional French cream cheese–based dessert.

7. Sifter
Turning the handle passes flour through the sifter's fine-mesh screen, giving it a uniform consistency for even blending. May also be used for sifting together several dry ingredients.

8. Springform Pan
Circular pan with spring-clip side that loosens for easy unmolding of delicate cakes.

9. Pastry Brushes
In two sizes, for brushing on glazes or sauces when preparing fruit desserts. Choose brushes with fairly flexible, not-too-thick, natural bristles.

10. Pastry Bag and Tip
Plastic-lined cloth or all-plastic bag and stainless-steel tip enable easy, accurate piping of meringue, whipped cream or other toppings.

11. Baking Sheet
For baking meringues and other edible bases for fresh fruit desserts.

12. Baking Dishes
For holding a wide range of oven-baked fruit desserts. Have a variety of sizes and shapes on hand; select heavy-duty glazed porcelain, stoneware, earthenware or ovenproof glass.

13. Rolling Pin with Handles
Most commonly used rolling pin for doughs. Choose one with ball-bearing handles for smooth rolling, and a hardwood surface at least 12 inches (30 cm) long. To prevent warping, do not wash; wipe clean with a dry cloth.

14. Assorted Utensils
Crockery jar holds wooden spoons for stirring; wire whisks for whipping egg whites and cream and for stirring and blending; rubber spatulas for folding and spreading; and a slotted spoon for simultaneously transferring and straining ingredients.

15. Food Mill
Hand-turned crank forces fruit through one of two disks to form coarser or finer purées while straining out peels, seeds and fibers.

16. Steamed Pudding Mold
Decorative tubed mold with lid, for containing puddings that cook in a water bath.

17. Kitchen Towel
Good-quality cotton towel for covering filo dough to prevent drying out; for removing the skins of hazelnuts (filberts); for forming rolled cakes; and for general kitchen cleanup.

Basic Meringue

This recipe can be used to make 3 large meringues for stacking with layers of whipped cream and fruit in between and on top, such as for the blackberry-strawberry meringue shortcake on page 43. It can also be used to make individual meringues that can be topped with whipped cream and fruit. Broken meringues taste wonderful folded into whipped cream or fruit fools. Use a perfectly clean bowl for whipping the egg whites, or they may not whip properly.

6 egg whites
¼ teaspoon cream of tartar
1 cup (8 oz/250 g) sugar

Position 2 racks in the lowest portion of an oven and preheat the oven to 300°F (150°C). Line 2 baking sheets with parchment paper or aluminum foil. Depending upon whether you are making individual meringues or large layers, draw eight 4-inch (10-cm) or three 8-inch (20-cm) circles on the lined sheets.

Place the egg whites in a bowl. Using an electric mixer, beat until well mixed. Sprinkle on the cream of tartar and continue beating until white and foamy. Very gradually add the sugar and continue beating until stiff, shiny peaks form. This whole process will take about 4 minutes.

To make individual meringues, spoon the egg whites onto the prepared baking sheets, filling the circles drawn on the sheets and forming eight 4-inch (10-cm) rounds. Build up the edges slightly. Alternatively, working in 3 batches, fill a pastry bag fitted with a large plain tip with the egg whites and pipe the 4-inch (10-cm) rounds onto the sheets in tight spirals, again building up the edges.

For 3 large layers, spoon the egg whites onto the prepared baking sheets, filling the circles drawn on the sheets and forming three 8-inch (20-cm) rounds. Build up the edges slightly. Alternatively, working in 3 batches, fill a pastry bag fitted with a large plain tip and pipe the meringue in a tight spiral, filling the 3 circles outlined on the baking sheets and building up the edges of each one.

Bake until firm and dry, about 1 hour. Turn off the oven and open the door. When the meringues are completely cool, remove them from the oven and peel off the parchment or foil. The meringues can be used immediately or stored uncovered for several days in a dry place (not refrigerated) on a rack so that air can circulate around them. If humid weather softens the meringues, dry them in a 150°F (66°C) oven for 10 minutes and leave them to cool completely in the turned-off oven until ready to serve.

Makes three 8-inch (20-cm) meringues, or eight 4-inch (10-cm) meringues

1. Beating the egg whites.
Put the egg whites in a mixing bowl and beat with an electric beater until well mixed. Add the cream of tartar and beat until white and foamy. Gradually add the sugar and beat until whites form stiff, shiny peaks when the beaters are lifted out.

2. Spooning the circles.
Line a baking sheet with parchment paper or aluminum foil and draw uniform circles the size of the desired meringues. Spoon the beaten egg whites evenly into the circles, forming slightly raised rims.

Piping the circles.
Alternatively, spoon the beaten egg whites into a pastry bag fitted with a large plain tip and pipe onto the paper or foil, starting at the center of each circle and spiraling outward. At the edge, apply more pressure on the bag to form a slightly raised rim.

3. Baking the meringues.
Bake the meringues in a preheated 300°F (150°C) oven until firm, dry and lightly colored, about 1 hour. Turn off the oven, open its door and leave the meringues inside until completely cooled. Carefully peel from parchment or foil.

Orange Sponge Cake

You can make a quick dessert with this versatile recipe: Bake the cake in a springform pan, pile with fresh fruit—sliced peaches, figs, berries or kiwifruits—and then brush the fruit with red currant glaze (recipe on page 12). If you like, crown it with whipped cream. Baked as a sheet cake, it can be cut into thirds and layered with fruit and whipped cream, or it can be left uncut, spread with fruit and whipped cream and rolled jelly-roll fashion. The cake can also be baked and then well wrapped and frozen for up to 3 months. Thaw at room temperature, then unwrap and top or layer with fruit; do not, however, attempt to fill and roll a thawed cake.

1 cup (3 oz/90 g) cake (soft-wheat) flour, sifted
    before measuring
1 teaspoon baking powder
¼ teaspoon salt
3 eggs
¾ cup (6 oz/185 g) granulated sugar
2 tablespoons orange-flavored liqueur
1 tablespoon orange juice, preferably freshly squeezed
½ cup (2 oz/60 g) confectioners' (icing) sugar, if
    making a sheet cake

Preheat an oven to 375°F (190°C). Grease a 10-inch (25-cm) springform pan or a 10-by-15-inch (25-by-37.5-cm) jelly-roll pan with butter or margarine, or spray with vegetable cooking spray. Line the bottom of the pan with parchment or waxed paper. Grease or spray again, then dust with flour, shaking out any excess flour.

Resift the flour together with the baking powder and salt into a bowl. Set aside.

Place the eggs in another bowl. Using an electric mixer set on high speed, beat until thick, about 4 minutes. Gradually adding the granulated sugar, 1 tablespoon at a time, continue beating at high speed. When all the sugar has been added, reduce the speed to low, add the liqueur and orange juice and beat only until mixed. Then, using a rubber spatula, fold in the flour mixture just until the flour disappears. Gently transfer the batter to the prepared pan, spreading it evenly.

If using a springform pan, place in the lower third of the oven and bake until the top is golden and a toothpick inserted in the center comes out clean, about 20 minutes. Let cool for 10 minutes. Run a knife around the edges of the cake and then release the sides of the pan. Invert a serving dish on the cake, then, holding the plate and the pan bottom together firmly, invert them. Lift off the pan bottom. (Use the tip of a knife, if necessary, to loosen the pan.) Peel off the paper while the cake is still warm.

If baking a sheet cake, place on the center rack of the oven and bake until the top springs back when touched in the middle, about 12 minutes; do not overbake. Sprinkle a clean kitchen towel with the confectioners' sugar and invert the pan atop the towel. Lift off the pan, tapping it first if necessary to release the cake. Peel off the waxed paper. Trim the edges of the cake to form a neat rectangle. To use for a layer cake, let cool completely on a wire rack, then cut into 2 or 3 rectangles.

To fill and roll the sheet cake, starting from a long side, roll up the cake and towel together. Transfer to a wire rack to cool completely. Gently unroll, spread with the desired filling and roll up again without the towel.

Makes one 10-inch (25-cm) round cake, or one 10-by-15-inch (25-by-37.5-cm) sheet cake

Praline Cups

Just about any fruit tastes delicious spooned into these crisp, nutty cups. Top with ice cream or whipped cream, if you like, for a showy instant dessert. Let the filled cups sit for about 10 minutes before serving, to soften them for easier eating. Serve with a knife and fork. The timing in this recipe is critical. It is best to bake two cups at a time, so that you can mold them into shape at just the right moment. The cups will keep for 1 week in a tightly covered container at room temperature.

unsalted butter, softened, for greasing aluminum foil
   and cups
1 cup (5 oz/155 g) all-purpose (plain) flour
1 cup (4–5 oz/125–155 g) finely chopped almonds
   or pecans
½ cup (4 fl oz/125 ml) corn syrup
½ cup (4 oz/125 g) unsalted butter
⅔ cup (5 oz/155 g) firmly packed dark brown sugar

Position a rack in the center of an oven and preheat the oven to 375°F (190°C). Cut aluminum foil into twelve 8-inch (20-cm) squares and grease with butter or spray with vegetable cooking spray. Place 2 foil squares on a baking sheet. Grease the outside bottoms and three-fourths of the way up the sides of 2 custard cups or flat-bottomed ½-cup (4-fl oz/125-ml) measuring cups.

In a bowl, stir together the flour and nuts; set aside.

In a small saucepan, combine the corn syrup, the ½ cup (4 oz/125 g) butter and the brown sugar. Bring to a boil over medium-high heat, stirring gently. Stir in the flour and nuts, then remove from the heat. Drop 2 rounded tablespoons of the mixture onto the center of each prepared foil square on the baking sheet.

Bake for 7 minutes. The praline should have bubbled and spread out into 4–5-inch (10–13-cm) rounds. Remove from the oven and let cool on the sheets for 2 minutes. Place 1 of the greased custard cups or measuring cups in the center of each praline circle.

Holding the cup in place, lift up the foil and gently mold the praline to the outside of the cup.

Cool upside down for 3 minutes, then remove the greased cups. Let the praline cups cool completely and then remove the foil. While the praline cups are cooling, repeat with the remaining praline mixture, regreasing the cups as necessary. If the praline mixture hardens, reheat gently over low heat until softened.

Makes 12 praline cups

1. Spooning the mixture.
Prepare the praline mixture as directed in the recipe. Drop 2 rounded tablespoons onto the center of a greased 8-inch (20-cm) square of aluminum foil. Bake in a preheated 375°F (190°C) oven for 7 minutes.

2. Forming a cup.
Let the praline cool for 2 minutes. Place the greased bottom of a measuring or custard cup in its center and lift the foil to mold the praline. Invert and cool 3 minutes; then remove the greased cup and peel off the foil.

FINISHING TOUCHES

Some fruits, because of the intensity of their flavor and color, display a natural affinity for garnishing other fruits. The four recipes that follow rely on the sharp flavor and ruby hue of red currant jelly, the vivid juiciness of raspberries and blueberries, and the pungency of orange peel to provide elegant finishing touches to fruit desserts.

Red Currant Glaze

This beautiful, translucent glaze will turn many fruit desserts into works of art. It can be stored in a tightly covered container in the refrigerator for several months. Reheat over low heat.

1 jar (8 oz/250 g) red currant jelly
¾ cup (5½ oz/170 g) superfine (caster) sugar
juice of 1 lemon
2 tablespoons kirsch or other fruit-flavored liqueur, optional

*I*n a small saucepan over medium heat, combine the jelly, sugar, lemon juice and liqueur (if using). Stir with a wire whisk until the mixture begins to bubble, then continue stirring until the sugar dissolves and the jelly is fully melted.

Remove from the heat and let cool for 15 minutes before using. Drizzle the glaze onto the dessert or apply with a pastry brush.

Makes about 1 ½ cups (12 fl oz/375 ml)

Raspberry Sauce

Fresh or frozen raspberries can be used for making this rich-colored sauce. Fresh raspberries will retain their full flavor because the sauce is uncooked. If frozen raspberries are used, they do not need to be thawed before combining with the currant jelly. The sauce can be refrigerated for 3 weeks or frozen for up to 2 months.

⅓ cup (3½ oz/105 g) red currant jelly
2 cups (8 oz/250 g) fresh or frozen raspberries

*I*n a small nonmetal bowl, melt the currant jelly in a microwave oven set on high power for 1 minute. Alternatively, in a small saucepan over medium heat, warm the jelly until it is fully melted, 2–3 minutes.

Place the raspberries in a bowl, stir in the melted jelly and let cool to room temperature.

Makes 2 ⅓ cups (19 fl oz/580 ml)

Blueberry Sauce

Made with fresh or frozen blueberries, this handy sauce will add a touch of class and a wonderful flavor to many desserts. Serve it hot, warm or cold. Store in a tightly covered container in the refrigerator for up to 2 weeks.

¼ cup (2 oz/60 g) sugar
2 tablespoons cornstarch
2 cups (8 oz/250 g) fresh or frozen blueberries
¼ cup (2 fl oz/60 ml) crème de cassis
¼ cup (2 fl oz/60 ml) orange juice, preferably freshly
   squeezed
juice of 1 lemon, or to taste

*I*n a small bowl, stir together the sugar and cornstarch. In a small saucepan over medium heat, combine the berries, liqueur and orange juice. Cook, stirring constantly, until the berries release their liquid. Remove from the heat and stir in the sugar-cornstarch mixture. Return the pan to low heat and cook, stirring constantly, until the mixture thickens slightly and is no longer cloudy, 3–4 minutes. Stir in the lemon juice.

Makes about 2⅓ cups (19 fl oz/580 ml)

Candied Orange Peel

Candied peel makes an attractive, tasty garnish for a variety of fruit desserts. In addition to navel oranges with Grand Marnier (recipe on page 78), sprinkle this peel on rubies in the snow (page 15) or on your favorite fruit desserts such as fools, mousses or salads. Other citrus peels—grapefruit, lime, lemon—can be candied in the same way.

1 large navel orange
½ cup (4 oz/125 g) sugar
2 tablespoons water

*U*sing a citrus zester, shave thin strips of the orange zest from the orange. Alternatively, use a small, sharp knife to cut thin strips of zest, then slice thinly. Be careful to remove only the bright orange surface of the peel, with none of the bitter white pith. Reserve the orange for another use.

  In a 1-qt (1-l) saucepan over medium-high heat, combine the sugar and water. Bring to a boil without stirring. Shake the pan if necessary to mix the sugar and water together. Add the orange zest strips and reduce the heat to medium-low. Cook, uncovered, stirring occasionally with a fork to be sure all the strips are coated with the syrup, until the sugar starts to crystallize around the edge of the pan, about 15 minutes.

  Remove from the heat. Using a fork, lift out the zest strips and arrange them in swirls and curves on a sheet of aluminum foil; do not touch the hot strips with your fingers. Let cool completely.

  Transfer to a container with a tight-fitting lid and store for up to several months.

Makes 16–20 strips

Rubies in the Snow

FOR THE WHITE CHOCOLATE CREAM:

2 cups (16 fl oz/500 ml) heavy
   (double) cream

4 oz (125 g) white chocolate, grated
   or finely chopped

4 egg whites from extra-large eggs

1 teaspoon vanilla extract (essence)

1 jar (10 oz/315 g) best-quality
   strawberry preserves

¼ cup (2 fl oz/60 ml) Grand Marnier
   or kirsch

4 cups (1 lb/500 g) stemmed *fraises
des bois* or small, native strawberries

Aromatic fraises des bois, *or wild strawberries, are rarely found in stores but are easy to grow in your garden. If you cannot find them, substitute cultivated strawberries, preferably the smaller native variety, which tend to be sweeter. This dessert looks beautiful garnished with candied violets, available in many specialty-food shops. Or simply top each serving with a fresh mint leaf.*

To make the white chocolate cream, pour 1 cup (8 fl oz/250 ml) of the cream into a small saucepan and place over medium heat. When tiny bubbles form around the edge of the pan, remove from the heat and whisk in the white chocolate. Pour the mixture through a sieve into a pitcher to rid it of lumps.

Combine the remaining 1 cup (8 fl oz/250 ml) cream and the egg whites in a heatproof 1-qt (1-l) bowl set over, but not touching, gently simmering water, or in the top pan of a double boiler set over simmering water. Dribble in the white chocolate cream, whisking constantly. Continue cooking, stirring constantly, until the mixture coats a spoon, 5–6 minutes. Transfer the bowl to a large bowl half full of ice water. Cover with plastic wrap, pressing it directly onto the surface to prevent a skin from forming. Let cool, stirring once after 10 minutes; this will take about 20 minutes. Stir in the vanilla, cover and chill well.

Place the preserves in a small saucepan over low heat until softened to a glaze, just a few minutes. Alternatively, put the preserves in a nonmetal dish and place in a microwave oven set on high power until softened to an almost liquid state or glaze, about 90 seconds. Stir in the liqueur, then cool for 2–3 minutes.

Spoon the white chocolate cream into 6–8 bowls or wineglasses. Top with the berries and the glaze and serve at once.

Serves 6–8

Summer Fruits in White Chocolate–Lime Sauce

12 oz (375 g) white chocolate, chopped into ½-inch (12-mm) pieces

2 cups (16 fl oz/500 ml) heavy (double) cream

2 teaspoons grated lime zest or 1 teaspoon lime oil (*see glossary*)

4 cups (1 lb/500 g) sliced assorted ripe summer fruits such as apricots, nectarines and peaches (½-inch/12-mm slices)

2 cups (8 oz/250 g) assorted berries such as raspberries, blackberries, strawberries and gooseberries

curls of lime zest or fresh mint sprigs for garnish

Use only the best-quality white chocolate and sweet ripe fruits. The sauce can be made up to 3 days ahead, covered and refrigerated. Soften it in a microwave oven or in the top pan of a double boiler or a heatproof bowl placed over (not touching) barely simmering water.

❧

Place the white chocolate in a food processor fitted with the metal blade or in a blender. Pour the cream into a small saucepan and place over medium heat. When tiny bubbles begin to appear around the edge of the pan, remove from the heat and pour the cream over the chocolate. Process until smooth. Add the lime zest or lime oil and process for a few seconds longer. Let cool to room temperature. The sauce should have the consistency of a very thick cream.

Arrange the fruit on a rimmed serving plate or in a bowl. Pour the cooled sauce over the fruit and garnish with lime zest curls or mint sprigs.

Serves 6–8

Melba Summer Pudding

1½ lb (750 g) peaches
juice of 1 lemon
3 cups (12 oz/375 g) fresh raspberries
    or 1 package (12 oz/375 g) frozen
    raspberries, slightly thawed
½ cup (4 oz/125 g) sugar
8 slices slightly stale challah or other
    rich, slightly sweet egg bread, crusts
    removed
⅓ cup (3 fl oz/80 ml) heavy (double)
    cream mixed with ¼ teaspoon vanilla
    extract (essence), optional
2 teaspoons unsalted butter or
    margarine, at room temperature
generous ⅓ cup (3 fl oz/80 ml) red
    currant glaze (recipe on page 12),
    optional
whipped cream for garnish, optional
fresh raspberries for garnish, optional
fresh mint leaves for garnish, optional

Traditionally this English pudding calls for soaking the bread in milk or cream. In this lighter version, the bread is merely brushed with cream—an optional step.

*B*ring a saucepan three-fourths full of water to a boil. Immerse the peaches for 30 seconds, then transfer to a work surface using a slotted spoon. When cool enough to handle, slip off the skins. Halve, pit and slice the peaches. Place in a bowl and toss with the lemon juice. Set aside.

In another bowl, toss together the raspberries and sugar. Brush both sides of each bread slice with the cream-vanilla mixture, if desired. Heavily grease a 2-qt (2-l) mixing bowl or pudding mold with the butter or margarine. Line with 6 of the bread slices, over-lapping them slightly and leaving a small opening in the bottom.

Spoon about 3 tablespoons of the raspberries into the bread-lined mold. Add a layer of peaches, then top with more of the raspberries. Repeat the layers until the fruits are used up. Place the remaining 2 bread slices on top, piecing as needed to cover completely. Cover with plastic wrap and weight with a small plate that fits inside the mold, pressing firmly to compress the pudding. Place a 1-lb (500-g) weight on the plate and refrigerate for 24 hours.

Remove the weight, plate and plastic wrap. Dip the mold in very warm water, almost to the rim, for about 45 seconds, then loosen the edges with a knife. Invert onto a serving plate.

If desired, brush the top and sides of the pudding with the red currant glaze. Garnish with the whipped cream, raspberries and mint leaves (if desired). Slice and serve.

Serves 6–8

Apricot Fool

1 lb (500 g) apricots

⅓–½ cup (3–4 oz/90–125 g) firmly packed dark brown sugar

1 cup (8 fl oz/250 ml) heavy (double) cream

A fool is an old-fashioned English dessert that combines puréed fruit and whipped cream or custard. This version is best when made with ripe fresh apricots. Canned apricots can also be used; drain them and reduce the sugar to ¼ cup (2 oz/60 g). Praline cups (recipe on page 11) filled with apricot fool and decorated with reserved apricot slices and additional whipped cream make a tasty and attractive presentation.

Halve and pit the apricots, then thinly slice them. It is not necessary to peel them. Set aside about 1½ cups (9 oz/280 g) of the apricot slices. Place the remaining apricot slices and the brown sugar in a food processor fitted with the metal blade or in a blender. The amount of sugar you use will depend upon how sweet the apricots are. Process until smooth.

Using chilled beaters and a large chilled bowl, whip the cream until stiff peaks form. Gently fold in the apricot mixture and then 1 cup (6 oz/185 g) of the reserved slices.

Spoon the apricot-cream mixture into individual bowls. Garnish with the reserved slices and serve.

Serves 4

Mango Mousse

1 lb (500 g) mangoes

½ cup (4 oz/125 g) sugar

1 envelope unflavored gelatin
  (1 tablespoon/¼ oz/7 g)

3 tablespoons water

1 cup (8 fl oz/250 ml) heavy (double)
  cream

3 cups (12 oz/375 g) fresh raspberries
  or 1 package (10 oz/315 g) frozen
  raspberries, thawed

Mangoes and raspberries are a wonderful combination, further enhanced here with rich cream. Choose only ripe, sweet, juicy mangoes for maximum flavor. They should be soft but not shriveled, and when they are sliced they should resemble the juiciest of peaches. The mousse will keep for 1 day without losing its volume. It can also be made ahead, layered with the raspberries, covered tightly and frozen for up to 1 week; thaw in the refrigerator before serving.

Peel the mangoes. Slice as much of the flesh off the pit as possible, being careful to capture any juices. Pass the mango pieces through a food mill held over a bowl, to form a smooth purée. Alternatively, press the mango flesh through a sieve into a bowl. Add any captured juice to the bowl as well. Add the sugar and set aside, stirring occasionally until the sugar dissolves completely in the juices.

In a small saucepan over low heat, stir the gelatin into the water to dissolve completely; do not allow to boil. Alternatively, in a small nonmetal bowl, stir the gelatin into the water and place in a microwave oven set on low power for 3 minutes to dissolve the gelatin completely. Let the mixture cool for 2–3 minutes, then stir into the mango purée.

Using chilled beaters and a large chilled bowl, whip the cream until stiff peaks form. Fold a quarter of the mango purée into the cream to lighten it. Then gently fold in the remaining mango purée just until combined.

Alternate layers of raspberries and mango mousse in 4 individual bowls or in a 1½-qt (1.5-l) serving bowl. Chill for at least 1 hour before serving.

Serves 4

Fruit Frappé

3 cups (1 lb/500 g) cut-up banana, mango, strawberries and/or papaya, in any combination (1½-inch/4-cm chunks)

1 cup (8 fl oz/250 ml) orange, pine-apple, grapefruit or cranberry juice, or as needed

1 cup (8 fl oz/250 ml) strawberry, lemon, lime, passion fruit or raspberry frozen yogurt or sherbet (low or nonfat)

More than just a sippable dessert, this refreshing treat is good for breakfast or as a cooling midday snack. It also makes a great starter for brunch. Garnish with sprigs of mint or attractively cut pieces of whatever fruit you use.

Place the fruit, juice and frozen yogurt or sherbet in a blender. Purée until smooth, adding additional juice if desired for a thinner consistency.

Pour into 4 glasses and serve immediately.

Serves 4

Lemon-Raspberry Mousse

1 envelope unflavored gelatin
  (1 tablespoon/¼ oz/7 g)
3 tablespoons water
⅓ cup (3 fl oz/80 ml) fresh lemon juice
  (about 3 lemons)
1 cup (8 oz/250 g) sugar
4 egg whites
2 teaspoons grated lemon zest
1 cup (8 fl oz/250 ml) heavy (double)
  cream
raspberry sauce *(recipe on page 12)*

For an elegant presentation, garnish this cool, refreshing dessert with whole fresh raspberries or thin slivers of lemon zest. The mousse will keep for 1 day in the refrigerator.

*I*n a small nonmetal bowl, stir the gelatin into the water. Add the lemon juice and sugar. Place in a microwave oven set on low power for 3 minutes to dissolve the gelatin completely. Alternatively, in a small saucepan, stir the gelatin into the water, add the lemon juice and sugar and place over low heat until the gelatin and sugar are fully dissolved. Do not let the mixture boil. In both cases cool the mixture to room temperature.

In a large bowl, beat the egg whites until soft peaks form. Beating continuously, add the gelatin mixture in a thin, steady stream. Continue to beat until stiff peaks form. Gently fold in the lemon zest.

Using chilled beaters and a chilled bowl, beat the cream until stiff peaks form. Fold the cream into the egg white mixture.

Spoon half of the raspberry sauce in the bottom of 6 bowls. Top with half of the lemon mousse. Repeat the layers, then serve.

Serves 6

Tropical Papaya Boats

2 papayas, each about 6 inches (15 cm)
  long
juice of 1 small lime
2 kiwifruits, peeled and sliced crosswise
1 cup (6 oz/185 g) fresh pineapple
  chunks
1 mango
1 banana, peeled and sliced crosswise

For the best results, use peak-of-ripeness fruits for the sweetest flavor. The boats can be assembled up to 4 hours in advance of serving, covered with plastic wrap and refrigerated. If you do prepare the dessert ahead of time, sprinkle the bananas with lemon or lime juice to keep them from turning brown. Star fruits, if available, make a wonderful garnish. Also called carambola, the star fruit is a tropical yellow-green fruit that is generally available from late summer through winter.

Cut the papayas in half lengthwise and scoop out the seeds. Set one half on each individual plate, hollow side up. Sprinkle evenly with the lime juice.

Arrange the kiwi slices and pineapple chunks attractively in the papaya halves.

Peel the mango. Cut the flesh lengthwise off the pit in thick slices, cutting as close to the pit as possible. Add the mango slices and banana slices to the papaya halves and serve.

Serves 4

Raspberry-Blackberry Gratin

3 egg yolks from extra-large eggs
1 tablespoon water
½ cup (4 oz/125 g) sugar
½ cup (4 fl oz/125 ml) framboise
(raspberry brandy)
2 cups (16 fl oz/500 ml) heavy (double)
cream, chilled
3 cups (12 oz/375 g) raspberries
3 cups (12 oz/375 g) blackberries

This beautiful dish consists of summer berries and a simple French custard called a sabayon. You can use any berries you wish, but the combination of raspberries and plump, sweet blackberries is a showstopper. Make this in a shallow, rimmed ovenproof dish or in individual baking dishes. Plan on preparing the sabayon at least 4 hours before serving.

Combine the egg yolks, water and sugar in a metal bowl set over, but not touching, gently simmering water, or in the top pan of a double boiler set over simmering water. Whisk constantly until the mixture is foamy and begins to thicken slightly, 2–3 minutes. Immediately remove from the heat and strain into a 2-qt (2-l) metal bowl. (The use of a metal bowl will help to cool down the mixture more quickly.) Stir in the framboise, cover and refrigerate for at least 4 hours or overnight.

Just before serving, position the rack 3–4 inches (7.5–10 cm) from the heat source in a broiler (griller) and preheat the broiler.

Using chilled beaters and a large chilled bowl, whip the cream until stiff peaks form. Gently fold the cream into the chilled custard. Scatter all the berries over the bottom of a 2-qt (2-l) ovenproof baking dish with at least 1-inch (2.5-cm) sides. Place the dish on a heavy-duty baking sheet or in a shallow baking pan to make for easier removal from the broiler. Gently pour and spoon the custard over the berries.

Broil (grill) until the top is browned and bubbling, 1½–2 minutes. Serve immediately.

Serves 8

Mango-Lime Sorbet

2 mangoes
1½ cups (12 fl oz/375 ml) water
1 cup (7 oz/220 g) superfine (caster)
  sugar
1 teaspoon grated lime zest

This tropical dessert makes a memorable end to a casual summer meal, or an interesting break between courses of a formal dinner. Use only ripe mangoes to ensure the fullest flavor. You can make this sorbet in an ice cream maker or in your freezer.

Peel the mangoes. Slice as much of the flesh off the pits as possible. Reserve the pits. Place the flesh in a food processor fitted with the metal blade or in a blender. Set aside.

Combine the water, sugar and pits in a saucepan over medium heat. Bring to a simmer, stirring to dissolve the sugar, and simmer for 5 minutes.

Remove the pits from the syrup and discard. Add the syrup and lime zest to the mango in the food processor or blender. Process until smooth. Set aside to cool completely.

Pour and scrape the mixture into a shallow pan, cover with aluminum foil and place in the freezer for 30 minutes. Stir with a whisk or fork to aerate, re-cover and return to the freezer for 1 hour longer. If you want a smoother texture, aerate the mixture one more time and return it to the freezer for 1 more hour. Alternatively, pour and scrape the mixture into an ice cream maker and freeze according to manufacturer's instructions.

Spoon into small bowls to serve.

Serves 6

Blueberry Crisp

4 cups (1 lb/500 g) fresh or frozen
  blueberries
1 tablespoon fresh lemon juice
¾ cup (6 oz/185 g) firmly packed light
  brown sugar
½ cup (2½ oz/75 g) all-purpose (plain)
  flour
½ teaspoon ground cinnamon
¼ cup (2 oz/60 g) unsalted butter or
  margarine, at room temperature,
  cut into pieces
¾ cup (2½ oz/75 g) rolled oats

Tart blueberries and a slightly crunchy, sweet topping come together in this easy-to-make dessert. For maximum taste, try to find wild berries (fresh or frozen), rather than the cultivated ones. Terrific served with vanilla ice cream.

Position a rack in the center of an oven and preheat the oven to 375°F (190°C). Grease a shallow 1½-qt (1.5-l) baking dish with butter or margarine, or spray with vegetable cooking spray.

Spread the fresh or frozen blueberries evenly over the bottom of the prepared baking dish and sprinkle with the lemon juice.

In a bowl and using a fork, mix together the brown sugar, flour, cinnamon, butter or margarine and rolled oats until well combined. Sprinkle evenly over the blueberries.

Bake until the top is golden and the blueberries are bubbling, about 30 minutes. Transfer to a rack to cool. Serve hot or warm.

Serves 6

Frozen Peach Daiquiris

2 large peaches, unpeeled, cut into
   chunks (about 2 cups/12 oz/375 g)
1 can (6 fl oz/180 ml) frozen pink
   lemonade, softened but not liquefied
¾ cup (6 fl oz/180 ml) light rum
4 or 5 ice cubes
fresh mint sprigs for garnish

Look no further than the blender for an ice-cold solution to summer's dog days—and for a marvelous way to use summer's ripe peaches. Make virgin daiquiris by substituting orange juice or other fruit juice for the rum.

Place the peaches, lemonade and rum in a blender. Blend on high for 15 seconds. Add the ice, 1 or 2 pieces at a time, and process until the ice is crushed and the ingredients are incorporated, 30–40 seconds.

   Pour into 4 glasses, garnish with mint sprigs and serve immediately.

Serves 4

Strawberries Romanoff

4 cups (1 lb/500 g) strawberries

¼ cup (2 fl oz/60 ml) orange juice, preferably freshly squeezed

2 tablespoons sugar

2 tablespoons orange-flavored liqueur such as Grand Marnier or Curaçao

1 cup (8 fl oz/250 ml) best-quality vanilla ice cream

2 cups (16 fl oz/500 ml) heavy (double) cream

An eye-catching yet easy dessert that is the perfect ending to a summer meal. Prepare the strawberries at least 2 hours (or as long as 8 hours) before you plan to serve them. Make the cream topping at the very last minute.

Remove the stems from the strawberries, then cut the berries in half lengthwise. Place in a bowl and sprinkle with the orange juice, sugar and liqueur. Cover and refrigerate for at least 2 hours or for as long as 8 hours.

Just before serving, soften the ice cream in a microwave oven set on high power for 15–20 seconds. Alternatively, leave the ice cream at room temperature for 15–20 minutes to soften.

Using chilled beaters and a large chilled bowl, whip the cream until stiff peaks form. Beat in the softened ice cream.

Divide the strawberries and their juices among 8 bowls or wineglasses. Top each serving with a generous amount of the cream and serve immediately.

Serves 8

Pineapple Granita with Pomegranate Seeds

1 cup (8 fl oz/250 ml) unsweetened
   pineapple juice
1 cup (8 oz/250 g) sugar
2 cups (12 oz/375 g) chopped drained
   pineapple (fresh, canned or frozen)
seeds of 1 pomegranate

The pomegranate seeds sprinkled on top of this tartly sweet, frozen dessert look like tiny rubies. Fresh mint leaves or finely grated lime zest are other possible garnishes. If you cannot find a sweet, ripe pineapple, substitute canned or frozen pineapple. Make this granita in an ice cream maker or in your freezer.

*I*n a small saucepan over medium heat, combine the pineapple juice and sugar. Bring to a simmer, stirring constantly, just until the sugar dissolves. Remove from the heat and let cool for 15 minutes.

In a food processor fitted with the metal blade or in a blender, combine the pineapple and the juice-sugar mixture. Process until smooth. Pour and scrape the mixture into a shallow pan, cover with aluminum foil and place in the freezer for 30 minutes. Stir with a whisk or fork to aerate, re-cover and return to the freezer for 1 hour longer. If you want a smoother texture, aerate the mixture one more time and return it to the freezer for 1 more hour. Alternatively, pour and scrape the mixture into an ice cream maker and freeze according to manufacturer's instructions.

To serve, spoon into bowls or wineglasses and sprinkle with the pomegranate seeds.

Serves 6

Blackberry-Strawberry Meringue Shortcake

basic meringue (recipe on page 8)
2 cups (8 oz/250 g) strawberries
2 cups (8 oz/250 g) blackberries
3 tablespoons blackberry brandy or
　other sweet liquor
2 cups (16 fl oz/500 ml) heavy (double)
　cream
2–3 tablespoons confectioners' (icing)
　sugar

The berries in this recipe are left tart to contrast with the sweetened cream and meringue, but, if you like, add 3–4 tablespoons sugar to the berries. Cut-up nectarines, peaches or apricots can be substituted for the berries. Individual meringues, as shown here, can be used in place of the three large meringues and layered with cream and fruit as desired.

Prepare 3 meringue layers (or small individual meringues, if you prefer). Let cool completely.

Remove the stems from the strawberries and then slice the berries. Place in a bowl. If you prefer to have less seeds, press half of the blackberries through a sieve. Add all the blackberries to the strawberries and sprinkle with the blackberry brandy. Set aside.

Using chilled beaters and a large chilled bowl, whip the cream until soft peaks form. Sprinkle with the sugar and beat just until stiff peaks form.

Place a meringue layer on a serving plate. Spread with one-third of the whipped cream. Top with one-third of the berries. Place a second meringue layer on top and spread with one-half of the remaining cream and top with one-half of the remaining berries. Top with the third meringue layer and spread with the remaining cream, reserving a small amount for garnish. Top with the remaining berries and garnish attractively with the reserved cream.

Let stand for 10 minutes, then cut and serve.

Serves 6–8

Cherry Ricotta Shells

2 cups (1 lb/500 g) ricotta cheese
½ cup (2 oz/60 g) confectioners' (icing)
  sugar
1½ lb (750 g) cherries (about 4½ cups),
  stemmed
½ cup (5 oz/155 g) cherry or red
  currant jelly
2–3 tablespoons kirsch
6 cannoli shells, praline cups (*recipe on
  page 11*) or chocolate cups

*Here, fresh cherries are added to sweetened ricotta and served
in cannoli shells, praline cups or chocolate cups. Look for
cannoli shells in well-stocked food stores or Italian bakeries.
The chocolate cups are available in specialty-food shops and in
stores that sell fine chocolates.*

In a bowl, whisk together the ricotta and confectioners'
sugar until combined and softened; be careful not to
overmix or the ricotta will become runny.

Remove the pits from the cherries and cut the cherries in
half. Fold half of the cherries into the ricotta mixture. Place
the remaining cherries in a food processor fitted with the
metal blade or in a blender. Process until finely chopped.
Leave the cherries in the processor or blender container.

Put the jelly in a nonmetal dish and place in a microwave
oven set on high power until melted, about 1 minute.
Alternatively, in a small saucepan over medium heat, warm
the jelly until it melts, 2–3 minutes. Add the melted jelly
and the kirsch to the chopped cherries and process until
puréed.

Divide the purée evenly among 6 plates. Fill the shells or
cups with the ricotta-cherry mixture and place in the
center of the purée on each plate. Let the dessert stand for
10 minutes to allow the shells to soften slightly and the
flavors to blend. Serve with knives and forks.

Serves 6

Baked Fresh Figs in Port

12 slightly underripe large figs
6 oz (185 g) cream cheese, well chilled
1½ cups (12 fl oz/375 ml) port or
   medium-dry sherry
¾ cup (6 oz/185 g) sugar
juice of 1 lemon
finely julienned zest of 1 lemon
whipped cream or crème fraîche for
   topping, optional (*see glossary for
   crème fraîche recipe*)

The time for fresh figs is the end of the summer and early fall. Select figs that are firm to the touch. Use regular cream cheese for this dessert; the whipped kind will not work. Serve hot at the end of a light meal, or for an unexpectedly lovely teatime treat. It's also wonderful at brunch.

*P*osition a rack in the middle of an oven and preheat the oven to 450°F (230°C).

Slip the sharp tip of a teaspoon (a grapefruit spoon is good for this) into the bottom of each fig, making an incision. Using the same spoon, scoop up 1 tablespoon of the cream cheese and gently insert it into the fig.

Place the filled figs, stem sides up, snugly together in a baking dish with at least 3-inch (7.5-cm) sides. (A soufflé dish is a good choice.)

In a small saucepan, combine the port or sherry and sugar and cook over medium heat, stirring constantly, until the sugar dissolves. Continue to cook until the mixture reduces by half and begins to become syrupy, 15–20 minutes. Add the lemon juice and zest and cook for 1 minute longer. Pour the syrup over the figs.

Bake until the sauce is hot and just begins to bubble, about 15 minutes. Do not overcook or the figs will fall apart. Spoon the figs and some of the syrup into individual bowls. Serve hot or warm, garnished with a dab of whipped cream or crème fraîche, if you wish.

Serves 4

Mixed Summer Fruit Compote

2 lb (1 kg) mixed summer fruits such as
   pitted cherries, raspberries,
   blueberries, stemmed strawberries,
   red currants, loganberries,
   gooseberries, blackberries or pitted
   apricots, peaches or nectarines

¾ cup (5½ oz/170 g) superfine (caster)
   sugar

1½ cups (12 fl oz/375 ml) plus 2
   tablespoons water

1 tablespoon cornstarch

This recipe gives you the freedom to use the best of summer's fruit bounty. For a more complex-tasting sauce, substitute a fruit wine such as blueberry, cherry or raspberry for ¾ cup (6 fl oz/180 ml) of the water. You can serve the compote plain or garnished with a dollop of whipped cream or fruit-flavored vanilla yogurt.

Cut the larger fruits into smaller pieces; leave the berries whole. Set aside.

In a 2-qt (2-l) saucepan set over medium heat, combine the sugar and the 1½ cups (12 fl oz/375 ml) water. Stir until the sugar dissolves, then bring the liquid to a boil.

Add the fruits to the sugar syrup and lower the heat so that the mixture simmers. Cook until the fruit is soft but has not begun to disintegrate, 3–4 minutes. Using a slotted spoon, transfer the fruit to a serving bowl. Allow the liquid to continue to simmer.

In a small cup, stir together the cornstarch and the 2 tablespoons water. Whisk it into the simmering liquid. Stir constantly until the liquid is clear and has thickened slightly, 2–3 minutes. Remove from the heat and let cool for 15 minutes, then pour over the fruit.

Cover and chill well before serving. Spoon into shallow bowls to serve.

Serves 6

Cassis Coeur à la Crème

1 cup (8 fl oz/250 ml) heavy (double) cream
¾ lb (375 g) cream cheese, at room temperature
2 egg whites
¼ cup (2 oz/60 g) superfine (caster) sugar
blueberry sauce, chilled *(recipe on page 13)*
6 strawberries for garnish, optional

Coeur à la crème is a cream cheese–based dessert traditionally made in a special heart-shaped mold with holes in the bottom to drain off excess moisture. The molds can be purchased in fine cookware stores. Some cooks use a cheesecloth-lined strainer or woven straw basket in place of the china molds. The accompanying blueberry sauce is flavored with crème de cassis, a liqueur made from black currants, to give this classic dish a pleasing new twist. Raspberry sauce (recipe on page 12) would also be an excellent accompaniment.

Line six 1-cup (8-fl oz/250-ml) heart-shaped molds (see note above) with cheesecloth (muslin). Allow about 2 inches (5 cm) of cheesecloth to overhang the edges of the mold.

Using chilled beaters and a large chilled bowl, whip the cream until it holds soft peaks. Beat in the cream cheese until the mixture is smooth.

In another bowl and using a wire whisk, beat together the egg whites and sugar until the mixture holds stiff peaks. Fold the egg whites into the cream mixture. Divide the mixture evenly among the prepared molds. Gently press down on the tops to pack each mold well. Set the molds in a shallow roasting pan and cover the pan with plastic wrap. Place in the refrigerator to drain for at least 4 hours or for up to 12 hours.

To serve, invert an individual plate over each mold, then, holding the plate and mold together firmly, invert them. Lift off the molds and peel off the cheesecloth. Spoon the blueberry sauce over the hearts and garnish each with a strawberry, if desired.

Serves 6

51

Grilled Pound Cake with Raspberry Sauce

1 pound cake, at least 9 inches (23 cm) long

2–3 tablespoons unsalted butter or margarine, at room temperature (optional)

raspberry sauce, chilled (recipe on page 12)

Serve this wonderful dessert to top off a barbecue; a wire grilling basket makes turning the cake easy. If you prefer to prepare the cake slices in a broiler (griller), brush each slice on both sides with melted unsalted butter or margarine, place on the rack of a broiler pan and broil (grill), turning once, until lightly toasted, about 1 minute on each side. Blueberry sauce (recipe on page 13) or sweetened sliced strawberries, peaches or nectarines can be used in place of the raspberry sauce. Seek out a high-quality pound cake at your favorite bakery.

If you have not already prepared a charcoal fire for grilling, prepare one now, or preheat an electric or gas grill. Make sure the grill rack is clean so the cake does not absorb any flavors from the previously grilled foods.

Cut the pound cake into 12 slices, each ¾ inch (2 cm) thick, and place obliquely in the grilling basket or on the grill rack. Toast, turning once, until the pieces are darkened on the edges and the marks of the basket or grill rack begin to show, about 2 minutes on each side. Remove the slices from the grill and spread with butter or margarine, if desired.

Place the toasted slices on a platter or individual plates. Spoon the chilled raspberry sauce in a line across the slices and serve the cake warm.

Serves 6

African Fruit Salad

1 large papaya, 1 lb (500 g) or larger
2 mangoes, about 1 lb (500 g) each
1 large pineapple, 3–4 lb (1.5–2 kg)
2 large bananas

Here is a naturally sweet, refreshing dessert that is a common finale to dinner parties in former French West Africa. Use only the ripest, fullest-flavored fruits: bananas that have just turned yellow and only the sweetest pineapple. If you cannot find large-sized fruits called for in the recipe, equivalent weights of smaller fruits can be used. You can make the salad up to 4 hours ahead of time, then cover with plastic wrap and refrigerate. Add the bananas just before serving, however, or they will turn brown. The fruits must all be cut into very small pieces for the dish to be at its best.

Halve the papaya and scoop out its seeds; peel the halves. Cut the flesh into small pieces and place in a large serving bowl.

Peel the mangoes. Slice as much of the flesh off the pit as possible, being careful to capture any juices. Cut the flesh into small pieces. Add the pieces and their juices to the bowl holding the papaya.

Using a sturdy, sharp knife, cut the top and bottom off of the pineapple. Set the pineapple upright on a cutting board. Working from the top to the bottom, slice off the dark, prickly outside skin. Cut out any remaining eyes or dark spots. (A strawberry huller works well for this.) Cut the pineapple lengthwise into quarters, being careful to capture any juices. Cut lengthwise again to remove the tough inner core on each quarter. Cut the pineapple into small pieces, again being careful to capture any juices. Add the pineapple and juices to the other fruits. Toss well, cover and refrigerate until well chilled.

Just before serving, peel the bananas and cut into small pieces. Add to the bowl, toss well and serve.

Serves 8

Strawberry-Rhubarb Brown Betty

2 cups (4 oz/125 g) fine fresh bread crumbs

1 cup (7 oz/220 g) firmly packed light brown sugar

½ teaspoon ground nutmeg

½ cup (4 oz/125 g) unsalted butter or margarine, melted

2½ cups (12 oz/375 g) thinly sliced rhubarb

6 cups (1½ lb/750 g) sliced, stemmed strawberries

A springtime favorite when both strawberries and rhubarb are in season. Sweet strawberries and tangy rhubarb are baked between layers of bread crumbs and brown sugar with a hint of nutmeg. The bread-crumb mixture on the bottom soaks up the fruit juices, while the top gets crispy. It is important to use a shallow baking dish so the sugared bread crumbs have enough contact with the tart rhubarb to sweeten it. Be sure to use only the stalks of the rhubarb, as the leaves can be toxic.

Position a rack in the center of an oven and preheat the oven to 375°F (190°C). Grease a 2½-qt (2.5-l) shallow baking dish with butter or margarine, or spray with vegetable cooking spray.

In a bowl and using a fork, stir together the bread crumbs and brown sugar. Add the nutmeg and butter or margarine and stir until all the ingredients are evenly distributed. In another bowl, combine the rhubarb and strawberries and toss to mix. Sprinkle half of the crumb mixture in the bottom of the prepared dish. Spread the fruit mixture evenly over the top, then sprinkle with the remaining crumb mixture.

Bake until the top is golden and the fruits are bubbling, about 45 minutes. Let cool for 15 minutes before serving, or serve at room temperature.

Serves 8

Three-Berry Cobbler

FOR THE FILLING:
1½ cups (6 oz/185 g) strawberries
1½ cups (6 oz/185 g) raspberries
1½ cups (6 oz/185 g) blackberries
½ cup (4 oz/125 g) sugar

FOR THE BISCUIT TOPPING:
⅓ cup (3 oz/90 g) unsalted butter or
   margarine, at room temperature
⅓ cup (3 oz/90 g) sugar, plus 1–2
   teaspoons sugar, optional
2 cups (10 oz/315 g) all-purpose
   (plain) flour
½ teaspoon salt
1 teaspoon baking powder
½ cup (4 fl oz/125 ml) milk

Cobblers conjure up memories of irresistible aromas in warm, friendly kitchens. This one combines blackberries, raspberries and strawberries under a sweet biscuit crust.

*P*osition a rack in the center of an oven and preheat to 375°F (190°C). Grease a deep 1½- or 2-qt (1.5- or 2-l) baking dish with butter or margarine, or spray with vegetable cooking spray.

   To make the filling, remove the stems from the strawberries and then slice the berries. Place in the prepared baking dish. Add the raspberries and blackberries. Sprinkle the sugar over the berries and toss to mix. Set aside.

   To make the biscuit topping, combine the butter or margarine and the ⅓ cup (3 oz/90 g) sugar in a bowl. Using a wooden spoon, a whisk or an electric mixer set on medium-high speed, beat until fluffy, 3–4 minutes. In another bowl, sift together the flour, salt and baking powder. Add the flour mixture alternately with the milk to the butter mixture, stirring with a fork just until the flour disappears. Do not overmix or the biscuit topping will become heavy.

   Turn the dough out onto a floured work surface and roll out or pat into the shape and size of the baking dish. Lift the dough onto the baking dish to cover the fruit; it should reach just slightly short of the dish sides. Crimp or flute the edges of the dough to form an attractive rim. Cut several slits in the top for steam to escape. Sprinkle with 1–2 teaspoons sugar, if desired.

   Bake until the top is golden and the berries are bubbling, about 50 minutes. Transfer to a rack to cool. Serve hot, warm or at room temperature.

Serves 6–8

Fresh Peach Kuchen

1–2 tablespoons unsalted butter, softened, for greasing pan, plus ½ cup (¼ lb/125 g) unsalted butter, melted

all-purpose (plain) flour for dusting pan, plus 1½ cups (6 oz/185 g) all-purpose (plain) flour, sifted before measuring

2 lb (1 kg) ripe peaches

2 tablespoons fresh lemon juice

2 teaspoons baking powder

½ teaspoon salt

½ cup (4 oz/125 g) granulated sugar

2 extra-large eggs

2 tablespoons milk

grated zest of 1 lemon

FOR THE TOPPING:

½ cup (3½ oz/105 g) firmly packed dark brown sugar

½ teaspoon ground cinnamon

½ teaspoon ground ginger

whipped cream for topping, optional

A kuchen is a homey coffee cake that is perfect at teatime or brunch.

*P*osition a rack in the center of an oven and preheat the oven to 375°F (190°C). Grease a 9-inch (23-cm) springform pan with the 1–2 tablespoons butter, then dust it with the flour; tap out any excess flour.

Bring a saucepan three-fourths full of water to a boil. Remove from the heat and immerse the peaches in the water for 4–5 minutes. Transfer to a work surface using a slotted utensil. When cool enough to handle, slip off the skins. Halve and pit the peaches, then cut into slices ¾ inch (2 cm) thick. Place in a bowl, add the lemon juice and toss to coat. Set aside.

Into a bowl resift the 1½ cups (6 oz/185 g) flour together with the baking powder, salt and granulated sugar. In a separate bowl and using a fork or whisk, beat together the eggs and milk, then beat in the melted butter and lemon zest. Dribble this mixture into the flour mixture, stirring with a fork just to moisten the dry ingredients; do not overmix. Spread the batter in the prepared pan. Drain the liquid from the peaches, reserving the liquid, and arrange the slices in a spiral design atop the batter. Drizzle the peach liquid over the peaches.

To make the topping, in a bowl combine the brown sugar, cinnamon and ginger. Stir with a fork to mix, then sprinkle evenly over the peaches.

Bake until a knife inserted in the center comes out clean, about 35 minutes. Let cool on a wire rack for 15 minutes. Remove the pan sides and transfer to a serving plate.

Serve warm or at room temperature. Top each serving with whipped cream (if desired).

Serves 6

Nectarines Poached in Champagne

8 large nectarines, about 4 lb (2 kg)
16 amaretti
3 cups (24 fl oz/750 ml) Champagne or
   sparkling wine
⅔ cup (5 oz/155 g) sugar
raspberry sauce (*recipe on page 12*)

Midsummer, when nectarines are at their peak, is the best time to make this simple and elegant dessert. Select large, firm (but not green) nectarines with rosy gold skins. Substitute peaches if you wish, or use a mixture of both. Amaretti are Italian almond-flavored macaroons; look for them in Italian or other specialty-food stores.

Fill a large saucepan three-fourths full of water and bring to a rapid boil. Add the nectarines and reduce the heat to a bare simmer. Simmer, uncovered, for 2 minutes. Then, using a slotted spoon, transfer the fruit to a bowl of cold water. Slip off the skins. You may have to use a paring knife to remove any skin that does not come off easily.

Cut the nectarines in half and remove the pits. Place 1 cookie in each cavity left by the pit. Arrange the halves, cut sides down, in a single layer in a nonaluminum baking pan (you may have to use several pans). Pour the Champagne or sparkling wine evenly over the nectarines and sprinkle with the sugar. Place a piece of waxed paper or parchment over the fruit, being careful that it doesn't hang over the pan and touch the heat element. Place the pan over low heat and bring to a gentle simmer. Cook just until the nectarines are very tender but not falling apart, 15–20 minutes. Turn off the heat and let cool completely in the pan.

To serve, ladle raspberry sauce on the bottom of individual rimmed plates. Using a slotted spoon, carefully place 2 nectarine halves on top of the sauce. Dribble more raspberry sauce over the top and serve.

Serves 8

Strawberry Sponge Brûlée

orange sponge cake baked in 10-inch
  (25-cm) springform pan *(recipe on
  page 9)*
4 cups (1 lb/500 g) strawberries
1 tablespoon granulated sugar
1¼ cups (10 fl oz/310 ml) sour cream
⅓ cup (2½ oz/75 g) firmly packed dark
  brown sugar

Here is a great party dish that can be assembled earlier in the day and then placed under the broiler for a few minutes just before serving. Watch closely once it goes into the broiler, and remove it as soon as the brown sugar melts and bubbles. For a more dramatic presentation, decorate the brûlée with whipped cream and mint leaves in addition to the strawberries.

Prepare the sponge cake and place on a flameproof serving plate.

Reserve 1 cup (4 oz/125 g) of the prettiest strawberries for garnishing the top of the cake. Remove the stems from the remaining strawberries and slice the berries. Place in a bowl, sprinkle with the granulated sugar and toss gently to mix. Spread in an even layer over the top of the cake.

Spread the sour cream evenly over the berries and then sprinkle with the brown sugar. Cover and refrigerate for 1–4 hours. Don't worry if it does not look pretty at this point.

Preheat the broiler (griller). Cover the edge of the cake plate with aluminum foil. Place in the broiler 2–3 inches (5–7.5 cm) from the heat source and broil (grill) until the brown sugar just begins to bubble in several places over the top of the cake, 2–3 minutes. Watch constantly to make sure it does not burn; remove it from the broiler immediately once it is ready.

Cool for 5–10 minutes so the sugar hardens into a shiny crust. Garnish the cake with the reserved strawberries. Cut and serve at once.

Serves 8

Chantilly Bananas

1 cup (8 fl oz/250 ml) heavy (double)
  cream
2 tablespoons dark brown sugar
1 cup (8 oz/250 g) plain yogurt
1 lemon
4 bananas
1 tablespoon fresh lemon juice
8 praline cups (*recipe on page 11*)

The French term chantilly *describes sweetened and flavored whipped cream—in this case, paired with bananas. Praline cups make an attractive presentation, but small bowls can be used if you are short of time. You can ready the cream mixture and the lemon zest about 1 hour before serving. Bananas turn brown and get mushy when prepared ahead of time, so add them at the last minute.*

Up to 1 hour before serving, using chilled beaters and a large chilled bowl, whip the cream until stiff peaks form. In another bowl, stir together the brown sugar and yogurt. Gently fold the yogurt mixture into the whipped cream. Cover and refrigerate if not using immediately.

   Using a zester, cut the zest (yellow part only) from the lemon in long, fine strips. Alternatively, use a small, sharp knife to cut thin strips of zest, then slice thinly. Finely chop about half of the zest strips. If you are not serving the dish immediately, store the zest tightly covered in the refrigerator.

   Just before serving, peel and slice the bananas. Place in a bowl and sprinkle with the lemon juice and the 1 teaspoon chopped zest. Toss gently to mix. Fold the bananas into the cream-yogurt mixture.

   Pile into the praline cups and place on individual plates. Decorate with the zest strips and serve at once.

Serves 8

Baked Winter Fruit Salad

2½ cups (12 oz/375 g) mixed dried fruits such as apricots, apples, peaches, pears, figs, raisins and pitted prunes

2 navel oranges, peeled, sectioned and membranes removed

1¼ cups (10 fl oz/310 ml) medium-dry sherry

1 cup (8 fl oz/250 ml) apple cider or orange juice

1 cinnamon stick

heavy (double) cream or plain yogurt for topping

Fresh and dried fruits give flavor and texture to this homey dish. The fruits must be soaked overnight, so plan ahead when making this dessert. If you don't wish to use sherry, increase the apple cider or orange juice to 2¼ cups (18 fl oz/560 ml). Serve warm with thick sweet cream or yogurt spooned over the top.

Place all the fruits, the sherry and cider or orange juice in a large bowl. Toss to combine. Cover and let soak overnight at room temperature.

Position a rack in the center of an oven and preheat the oven to 350°F (180°C).

Pour and scrape the fruits and liquid into a 2-qt (2-l) baking dish. Add the cinnamon stick and cover the dish with aluminum foil.

Bake until the liquid is bubbling and the fruits are very soft, about 45 minutes. Remove from the oven and let cool slightly. Discard the cinnamon stick.

Spoon into individual bowls and serve. Pass the cream or yogurt.

Serves 4–6

Tapioca Brûlée with Sun-Dried Blueberries

2 eggs, lightly beaten
6 tablespoons (1½ oz/45 g) instant tapioca
1 can (14 fl oz/440 ml) sweetened condensed milk
2 cups (16 fl oz/500 ml) whole milk
1 teaspoon grated lemon zest or ½ teaspoon lemon oil (see glossary)
⅔ cup (3 oz/90 g) sun-dried blueberries
1 cup (7 oz/220 g) firmly packed dark brown sugar
2 tablespoons hot water

This new version of crème brûlée relies on an old and much beloved comfort dish: tapioca pudding. It uses instant tapioca, which delivers the same taste as the long-cooking type but in a fraction of the time. You may substitute sun-dried cherries or cranberries for the blueberries, or use a combination of the three. Do not make the topping until just before serving time, as the sugar layer will lose its wonderful brittleness upon sitting. For an even more delectable dish, serve with blueberry sauce (recipe on page 13).

*I*n a saucepan, combine the eggs, tapioca, condensed milk and whole milk. Stir with a whisk to mix and then let stand for 5 minutes. Place the pan over medium heat and stir slowly until the mixture comes to a full boil; this will take 5–7 minutes. Cook, stirring constantly, for 1 minute longer. The mixture will have thickened considerably. Stir in the lemon zest or lemon oil and the blueberries and pour the mixture into a shallow 1½–2-qt (1.5–2-l) flameproof dish. Chill, uncovered, until very cold.

Just before serving, position a rack in the highest point in the broiler (griller) and preheat the broiler. Place the brown sugar in a small bowl and stir in the hot water to make a very thick paste that is free of lumps. Using the back of a spoon, spread a thin layer of the sugar paste over the top of the chilled pudding. Broil (grill) until the sugar melts and starts to bubble, 1–2 minutes. Watch carefully so that it does not burn. Remove from the oven and let stand until the sugar hardens into a shiny crust, 5–10 minutes.

Spoon onto small individual plates and serve at once.

Serves 8

Banana Fritters

½ cup (2½ oz/75 g) all-purpose (plain) flour

pinch of salt

1 teaspoon baking powder

1 egg

1 tablespoon granulated sugar

1 tablespoon unsalted butter or margarine, melted

⅓ cup (3 fl oz/80 ml) milk

½ teaspoon grated lemon zest

vegetable oil for deep-frying

4 bananas

½ cup (2 oz/60 g) confectioners' (icing) sugar for topping, optional

The deep-golden-brown and crispy batter contrasts pleasingly with the sweet banana. The batter also works well with apples cut into rings, or finely chopped plums or kiwifruits.

Sift together the flour, salt and baking powder into a bowl. In another bowl, beat together the egg, granulated sugar, melted butter or margarine, milk and lemon zest. Add the flour mixture and stir until mixed.

In a deep frying pan or sauté pan, pour in oil to a depth of 1½ inches (4 cm) and heat the oil to 375°F (190°C), or until a bit of batter turns golden within a few moments of being dropped in the oil. Peel the bananas, cut in half lengthwise and then cut crosswise into 2-inch (5-cm) lengths. Spear a banana piece onto a fork, dip it into the batter and then tap the fork on the edge of the bowl to remove excess batter. Lower the banana into the hot oil and free it from the fork. Add additional banana pieces in the same manner, but do not crowd the pan. Spoon the hot oil over the bananas until they puff up, then fry until they are deep golden brown, 3–4 minutes. Using a slotted spoon, transfer to paper towels to drain. Repeat with the remaining banana pieces.

Serve warm, dusted with confectioners' sugar, if desired.

Serves 6

Texas Ruby Red Grapefruit Sorbet

¾ cup (6 oz/185 g) sugar

⅔ cup (5 fl oz/160 ml) water

3 tablespoons fresh lemon juice

finely grated zest of 1 Ruby Red
  grapefruit

1¼ cups (10 fl oz/310 ml) Ruby Red
  grapefruit juice, including the pulp
  but not the white membrane

Peak season for these huge, sweet grapefruits is winter through early spring. The color of the pulp is a dramatic deep pink, which gives a gorgeous rosy hue to the sorbet. If you cannot find Ruby Red grapefruits, choose any pink, very flavorful variety. Serve as a simple yet memorable finale to almost any meal. Or offer it between courses to refresh the palate. If you like, prepare candied grapefruit peel according to the directions on page 13 and use to garnish the dessert. This sorbet can be made either in your freezer or in an ice cream maker. The hand method will result in a sorbet with larger ice crystals. Either way, it is delicious.

In a small saucepan over medium heat, combine the sugar, water and lemon juice. Bring to a simmer, stirring constantly until the sugar dissolves, then simmer for 5 minutes. Remove from the heat and let cool completely.

In a bowl, combine the cooled syrup, grapefruit zest, juice and pulp. Cover and chill until very cold.

Pour the mixture into a shallow pan, cover with aluminum foil and place in the freezer for 20 minutes. Stir with a whisk or fork to aerate; re-cover and return to the freezer. Continue to stir every 20 minutes until the sorbet is frozen; it should take 2 hours in all. Alternatively, pour the chilled mixture into an ice cream maker and freeze according to manufacturer's instructions.

To serve, spoon into individual bowls or wineglasses.

Serves 4

Prunes in Armagnac with Crème Fraîche

2 navel oranges, unpeeled

3 cups (18 oz/560 g) pitted whole prunes

1 cup (8 fl oz/250 ml) Armagnac or other high-quality brandy

1 cup (8 fl oz/250 ml) orange juice, preferably freshly squeezed

½ cup (4 fl oz/125 ml) water

1 cinnamon stick

2 cups (16 fl oz/500 ml) crème fraîche (*see glossary for recipe*)

This is an adaptation of a famous recipe served in Gascony, a region of southwestern France where Armagnac—a smooth, dark aromatic brandy—is made. Candied oranges, sometimes called glacéed oranges, can be used in place of the fresh oranges. Look for high-quality candied oranges in specialty-food shops; use 1 cup (6 oz/185 g), cut into 2-inch (5-cm) pieces, and add them during the last 10 minutes of cooking. This dessert is traditionally served in a pitcher, with the prunes on the bottom and the cream on top, although it is equally sensational served in large wineglasses. You can prepare the prune mixture up to 3 weeks ahead of serving; store it in a covered container in the refrigerator.

Cut the oranges in half vertically. Cut each half crosswise into slices 1 inch (2.5 cm) thick or into wedges.

In a heavy-bottomed 1½-qt (1.5-l) saucepan, combine the oranges, prunes, brandy, orange juice, water and cinnamon stick. Place over medium heat, cover and bring to a boil. Reduce the heat to low and simmer covered, stirring gently every 10 minutes and adding more water if the pan becomes too dry, until the prunes are very soft and most of the liquid has been absorbed, 35–40 minutes. The liquid that remains should be very thick and syrupy. Remove from the heat and let cool to room temperature; cover and refrigerate until ready to serve.

To serve, discard the cinnamon stick. Spoon the fruit and the syrup into 6–8 wineglasses or bowls. Top with the crème fraîche and serve.

Serves 6–8

Navel Oranges with Grand Marnier

4 large navel oranges
½ cup (4 oz/125 g) sugar
2 tablespoons water
2–3 tablespoons Grand Marnier
candied orange peel (*recipe on page 13*)

Navel oranges, candied orange peel and a touch of Grand Marnier make a marvelous blend of different orange flavors. It is crucial to remove, along with the peel, all the white membrane and strings from the oranges.

Peel the oranges, being careful to remove all of the white membrane and any strings. Cut the oranges in half vertically and remove any white membrane on the cut surfaces. Cut the orange halves crosswise into slices ¼ inch (6 mm) thick and place in a serving bowl. Set aside.

In a small, heavy saucepan, combine the sugar and water. Place over medium-high heat and bring to a boil, without stirring, until bubbles cover the entire surface of the syrup. Boil for 1 minute longer and remove from the heat. Add the Grand Marnier to taste and stir to mix.

Pour the hot syrup over the orange slices and stir to mix. Garnish with the candied orange peel and serve.

Serves 6

Cherries Jubilee

¾ cup (3 oz/90 g) sun-dried cherries

¾ cup (6 fl oz/180 ml) kirsch

1 cup (8 fl oz/250 ml) orange juice,
preferably freshly squeezed

2 cans (16 oz/500 g each) pitted dark
sweet cherries

½ cup (4 fl oz/125 ml) orange-flavored
liqueur

1 cup (10 oz/315 g) currant jelly

1 tablespoon grated orange zest

1 qt (1 l) best-quality vanilla or cherry
ice cream

Dried and canned cherries make this a great cold-weather dessert—a taste of summer in the wintertime. Some preparation is done the night before. Grand Marnier, Curaçao, Cointreau or Triple Sec can be used for the orange-flavored liqueur. Or substitute orange juice for both the orange-flavored liqueur and kirsch. If you use only orange juice, however, you will not be able to flame the sauce.

The night before, place the sun-dried cherries, ¼ cup (2 fl oz/ 60 ml) of the kirsch and the orange juice in a small saucepan set over low heat. Cook, uncovered, until the cherries have softened slightly and begun to absorb the liquid; this will take several minutes. Remove from the heat, let cool, cover and let stand at room temperature overnight.

That same night, drain the canned cherries and place them in a bowl. Add the orange-flavored liqueur. Cover and let stand at room temperature overnight.

At serving time, place the currant jelly in a large sauté pan over medium heat. Stir until the jelly melts, 2–3 minutes. Add both the dried and canned cherries and their soaking liquids and the orange zest. Reduce the heat to low; when the mixture begins to simmer, cook for 5 minutes.

Divide the ice cream among 8–10 bowls. Pour the remaining ½ cup (4 fl oz/120 ml) kirsch into a small pan and warm it over low heat. Pour the warm kirsch over the cherries and ignite with a long kitchen match. Stir, or shake the pan back and forth over the burner, until the flames die down, then immediately spoon the hot cherries and sauce over the ice cream and serve.

Serves 8–10

Tart Tatin

3 tablespoons unsalted butter or
   margarine
½ cup (4 oz/125 g) sugar
6 Granny Smith or other firm tart
   apples, peeled, cored and thickly
   sliced
1 square puff pastry, 10 inches (25 cm),
   thawed if frozen

This version of the famous upside-down apple tart Tatin uses puff pastry. Look for puff pastry in the freezer section of well-stocked food stores or in food-specialty markets, or buy fresh puff pastry at a bakery. If using frozen pastry, follow the package directions for thawing. A dollop of whipped cream makes a nice topping.

*P*osition a rack in the center of an oven and preheat the oven to 350°F (180°C).

In a 10-inch (25-cm) cast-iron or other heavy ovenproof frying pan over medium-high heat, melt together the butter or margarine and sugar, stirring to prevent scorching. Heat until the syrup is a rich caramel color, about 8 minutes.

Reduce the heat to low. Add the apple slices, arranging them in a decorative swirl starting from the outside edges of the pan. Place the apple slices rounded sides down, because the tart will be turned upside down when it is served. Simmer, uncovered, until the apples are slightly tender yet still firm, about 10 minutes. Shake the pan occasionally to prevent scorching. Remove from the heat.

Trim the corners of the puff pastry to form a rough 10-inch (25-cm) circle. Place the pastry over the apples and, using the tip of a knife, push it down between the apples and the edge of the pan. Bake until the pastry is golden and puffed, about 20 minutes. Let cool for 10 minutes.

Using a knife, loosen the edges of the tart from the pan. Invert a serving plate over the pan and then, holding the pan and plate together firmly, invert them. Lift off the pan. Serve warm or at room temperature.

Serves 6

Pavlova

2 egg whites
1 teaspoon cornstarch
1 cup (8 oz/250 g) sugar
1 teaspoon fresh lemon juice
1 teaspoon vanilla extract (essence)
6 kiwifruits, about 1 lb (500 g) total
  weight
1 cup (8 fl oz/250 ml) heavy (double)
  cream

Both Australia and New Zealand claim credit for inventing this dessert, created to commemorate a visit by Russian ballerina Anna Pavlova. The baked meringue can be made several days ahead, then stored uncovered in a dry place (not refrigerated) on a rack so that air can circulate around it.

*P*osition a rack in the lower third of an oven and preheat the oven to 300°F (150°C). Line a baking sheet with aluminum foil or parchment paper. Draw a 9-inch (23-cm) circle on the foil or parchment.

In a bowl, beat the egg whites until well mixed. Sprinkle on the cornstarch and continue beating until white and foamy. Very gradually add the sugar and continue beating until stiff, shiny peaks form. Quickly beat in the lemon juice and vanilla.

Spread the meringue evenly inside the circle drawn on the foil or parchment, building up the edges slightly to form a rim. Alternatively, use a pastry bag fitted with a large star or plain tip to pipe a tight spiral of meringue.

Bake until crispy, about 40 minutes. Turn off the oven and open the door. When the meringue is completely cool, remove from the oven. Then remove from the foil or parchment and place the meringue on a serving plate.

Peel the kiwifruits and slice them ¼ inch (6 mm) thick; you should have about 2¼ cups. Set aside.

Using chilled beaters and a chilled bowl, whip the cream until stiff peaks form. Spread the cream evenly on the baked meringue. Arrange the kiwi slices in an attractive pattern on top. Let stand for 10 minutes to soften the center of the meringue slightly, then cut into wedges to serve.

Serves 6–8

Apples in Filo

⅔ cup (5 oz/155 g) sugar

½ teaspoon ground cinnamon

½ cup (4 oz/125 g) unsalted butter or margarine

½ cup (4 fl oz/125 ml) vegetable oil

1 package (1 lb/500 g) filo dough, thawed if frozen

8 apples, peeled and cored (*see note*)

vanilla ice cream, optional

If using frozen filo, read the package for directions on how to thaw the delicate sheets. It is critical to keep the sheets covered or they will quickly dry out. You will need 20 filo sheets; leftover sheets can be tightly wrapped in plastic wrap and refrozen. For a tart dessert, use Granny Smith apples; for a sweeter dessert, use McIntosh.

Position a rack in the middle of an oven and preheat the oven to 375°F (190°C). Grease a baking sheet with butter or margarine, or spray with vegetable cooking spray.

In a small bowl, stir together the sugar and cinnamon and set aside. In a small saucepan, melt together the butter or margarine and oil; set aside.

Remove 20 filo sheets from the package and, using scissors, cut the stack of sheets into quarters. Leave out one-quarter of the sheets and cover with plastic wrap. Return the rest of the filo to a sealed plastic bag.

Gently peel off 1 filo sheet and lay it on a work surface. Brush with the oil-butter mixture. Remove a second sheet, rotate it slightly and lay it obliquely on top of the first sheet. Brush with the oil-butter mixture. Continue layering the sheets, rotating slightly each time, until you have a stack of 10 sheets.

Place 1 apple in the center of the stack and spoon one-eighth of the sugar-cinnamon mixture into its center. Bring the edges up around the apple and pinch closed at the top. Transfer to the prepared baking sheet. Repeat with the remaining filo, apples, butter mixture and sugar mixture.

Bake until the dough is deep golden, the apples are soft and the center is bubbly, 40–45 minutes. Let stand 10 minutes, then serve with vanilla ice cream, if desired.

Serves 8

Cranberry-Apple Slump

1½ lb (750 g) Granny Smith or other firm tart green apples, peeled, cored and sliced (about 4 cups)

2 cups (8 oz/250 g) cranberries (fresh or frozen)

1 cup (8 oz/250 g) sugar

FOR THE BISCUIT TOPPING:

1¼ cups (6½ oz/200 g) all-purpose (plain) flour

2 teaspoons baking powder

½ teaspoon salt

⅓ cup (3 oz/90 g) unsalted butter or margarine, at room temperature

½ cup (4 fl oz/125 ml) milk

grated zest of 1 orange

Apples and cranberries have wonderfully complementary flavors. In this cobblerlike dessert they are baked with a biscuit topping. The juices from the cooked fruit bubble up through the nooks and crannies and are absorbed by the baked topping. A scoop of vanilla ice cream is a wonderful companion.

*P*osition a rack in the center of an oven and preheat the oven to 375°F (190°C).

In a large bowl, combine the apple slices and cranberries. Add the sugar and toss to mix. Scatter the fruit mixture evenly over the bottom of a large ovenproof frying pan. Place over medium heat and cook uncovered until the juices are bubbling, about 10 minutes.

Meanwhile, make the biscuit topping: Sift together the flour, baking powder and salt into a bowl. Add the butter or margarine and, using a pastry blender or 2 knives, cut it into the flour mixture until it is the consistency of coarse meal. Gradually add the milk, stirring with a fork until the flour disappears. Do not overmix or the biscuit topping will be heavy.

For cut biscuits, roll out the dough ¾ inch (2 cm) thick on a floured work surface. Using a biscuit cutter or a glass 2 inches (5 cm) in diameter, cut out biscuits. Place atop the apples and cranberries, arranging them evenly on the surface. Alternatively, if you prefer dropped biscuits, drop the flour mixture by heaping tablespoons onto the fruit.

Place the pan in the oven and bake until the biscuits are golden and the fruit is bubbly, about 35 minutes. Serve immediately or let cool on a wire rack to room temperature.

Serves 6

Chocolate-Dipped Frozen Bananas

1½ cups (7½ oz/235 g) hazelnuts (filberts)

12 oz (375 g) bitter or semisweet chocolate, chopped

¼ cup (2 oz/60 g) unsalted butter

4 large, firm bananas

A confection for children—and anyone who is still a child at heart.

Preheat an oven to 300°F (150°C). Spread the hazelnuts in a shallow pan and place in the oven until lightly toasted and the skins begin to loosen from the nuts, 10–12 minutes. Remove from the oven and pour the hot nuts into a kitchen towel. Rub the towel against the nuts to flake off as much of the skins as possible. Chop the nuts. Alternatively, place the toasted hazelnuts in a food processor fitted with the metal blade. Process with on-off pulses until the nuts are coarsely chopped, then pour into a large wire-mesh sieve and shake vigorously; the skins will flake off.

Place the chocolate and butter in a bowl set over (but not touching) gently simmering water, or in the top pan of a double boiler set over gently simmering water. Stir occasionally until the mixture is smooth. Remove from the heat, but leave over the hot water.

On a sturdy tray, set out about 40 fluted paper cups 2 inches (5 cm) in diameter. Sprinkle about 1 teaspoon of the chopped nuts into the bottom of each cup.

Peel the bananas and cut each one crosswise into 10 slices, each about 1 inch (2.5 cm) thick. Spear a slice onto a metal or wooden skewer and dip into the chocolate, coating it. Place in a paper cup and sprinkle with another 1 teaspoon or so of nuts. Repeat with the remaining banana slices, chocolate and nuts.

Place the tray in the freezer for at least 2 hours or as long as 24 hours. Thaw for 2 minutes before serving.

Makes about 40 slices

Bananas Foster

6 tablespoons (3 oz/90 g) unsalted
  butter
½ cup (3½ oz/105 g) firmly packed
  dark brown sugar
finely julienned zest of 1 lemon
½ teaspoon ground cinnamon
4 ripe bananas, peeled and halved
  lengthwise
1 pint (500 ml) best-quality vanilla
  ice cream
¼ cup (2 fl oz/60 ml) banana-flavored
  liqueur
⅓ cup (3 fl oz/80 ml) light or dark rum
2 tablespoons fresh lemon juice

Don't wait to go to New Orleans to enjoy this famous dessert created by the Brennan family and served in their restaurants there since its invention in the 1950s. The secret to getting the alcohol to ignite is to warm it first. This dish makes a spectacular presentation.

*I*n a chafing dish or a frying pan over medium heat, melt together the butter and brown sugar. Add the lemon zest and cook, stirring to blend the butter and sugar thoroughly, for 2 minutes. Stir in the cinnamon. Reduce the heat to low, add the bananas and cook, frequently spooning the hot sauce over them, until tender, 5–7 minutes; the timing depends upon how ripe the bananas are.

Just before serving, divide the ice cream among 4–6 bowls. Pour the liqueur, rum and lemon juice into a small saucepan and place over medium heat until warm. Alternatively, pour into a small nonmetal bowl and heat in a microwave oven set on high power until warm, about 40 seconds.

Bring the pan holding the bananas, the pan or dish of warmed spirits and the bowls of ice cream to the table. Pour the liqueur over the bananas and ignite with a long kitchen match. When the flames die out, spoon the bananas over the ice cream and serve.

Serves 4–6

Italian Plum Focaccia

1 tablespoon active dry yeast

½ cup (4 fl oz/125 ml) warm milk
  (120°F/49°C)

½ cup (4 oz/125 g) granulated sugar

¼ cup (2 oz/60 g) unsalted butter, very
  soft, plus 1½ tablespoons butter for
  greasing pan

2 extra-large eggs

2 teaspoons grated lime zest or
  1 teaspoon lime oil (*see glossary*)

½ teaspoon salt

½ cup (2½ oz/75 g) cornmeal

3 cups (15 oz/470 g) all-purpose
  (plain) flour, plus extra for sprinkling

vegetable oil for oiling bowl

8 Italian plums, cut in half and pitted

1 egg mixed with 1 tablespoon water

1–2 tablespoons coarse sugar

Use smallish, sweet purple Italian plums for this brunch showpiece.

Place the yeast, milk and 1 teaspoon of the granulated sugar in a large mixing bowl. Stir to dissolve the yeast. When creamy on top, after about 5 minutes, add the ¼ cup (2 oz/60 g) butter, the eggs, lime zest or lime oil, salt, cornmeal, flour and the remaining granulated sugar. Stir until a soft dough forms. Turn out onto a lightly floured surface and knead until smooth and no longer sticky, 5–8 minutes. Add more flour, if necessary, to keep the dough from sticking.

Form the dough into a ball and place in a well-oiled bowl. Turn the ball to coat with oil, cover the bowl with plastic wrap and set in a warm place to rise until doubled in bulk, about 1 hour. Alternatively, refrigerate the dough overnight.

Butter a heavy-duty baking sheet or pizza pan with the 1½ tablespoons butter. Punch down the dough and turn it out onto a lightly floured surface. Pat into an 11-inch (28-cm) round. Transfer to the prepared sheet. Using a finger, poke 16 holes about 1½ inches (4 cm) apart across the top of the dough. Insert a plum half, cut side up, into each hole. Push the fruits aggressively into the dough; they should rest in small indentations. Brush the top with the egg-water mixture and sprinkle with the coarse sugar. Let rise in a warm place until almost doubled in bulk, about 30 minutes.

Meanwhile, position a rack in the middle of an oven and preheat the oven to 400°F (200°C). Bake for 15 minutes. Reduce the heat to 350°F (180°C) and bake until golden brown, about 15 minutes longer. If it begins browning too much, cover with aluminum foil. Serve hot or warm.

Serves 10

Baked Apples with Mascarpone and Dried Apples

6 very large Granny Smith or other firm
   tart apples
½ cup (4 fl oz/125 ml) apple brandy,
   Calvados or apple cider
⅔ cup (2 oz/60 g) dried apples, cut into
   1-inch (2.5-cm) pieces
½ lb (250 g) mascarpone cheese
½ cup (3½ oz/105 g) firmly packed
   dark brown sugar

*This autumn dish combines the tartness of fresh apples, the sweetness
of dried apples and the creamy tang of mascarpone cheese—a soft,
rich Italian cream cheese available in specialty-food shops and Italian
stores. Apple brandy or Calvados—an exquisite apple brandy bottled
in Normandy—provides the perfect finish.*

*P*osition a rack in the center of an oven and preheat the oven
to 350°F (180°C).

Core each apple, cutting to within ¾ inch (2 cm) of the
bottom; be careful not to pierce the bottom. Remove a ring of
peel 1 inch (2.5 cm) wide from around the stem area. Trim a
little slice off the bottom if necessary for it to stand upright.
Scoop out a pocket 1½ inches (4 cm) wide and 2½ inches
(6 cm) deep from the center. (A grapefruit spoon works well
for this step.) Stand the apples upright in a shallow baking dish.

Place the brandy or cider and the dried apples in a small
saucepan over medium heat. Bring to a simmer, then simmer
gently, stirring occasionally, until the apples are soft and have
absorbed most of the liquid, 6–8 minutes. Remove from the heat
and stir in the mascarpone and brown sugar.

Spoon the cheese mixture into the center of the apples. Pour
water into the baking dish to a depth of 1 inch (2.5 cm). Bake
until tender when pierced, about 30 minutes.

Transfer the apples to individual shallow bowls. Spoon any
liquid in the pan over the apples. Serve hot, warm or at room
temperature.

Serves 6

Hungarian Apricot Crêpes

FOR THE CRÊPES:

¾ cup (4 oz/125 g) all-purpose (plain) flour

2 tablespoons sugar

¼ teaspoon salt

1 extra-large egg, plus 1 egg yolk

1½ cups (12 fl oz/375 ml) milk

1 tablespoon unsalted butter, melted, plus 2–3 tablespoons butter for cooking the crêpes

1½ cups (15 oz/470 g) best-quality apricot preserves

3 tablespoons unsalted butter

¼ cup (2 fl oz/60 ml) amaretto, apricot brandy or orange juice

½ cup (2 oz/60 g) finely chopped walnuts

You can make these delicate crêpes the day before serving: Stack between sheets of plastic wrap or waxed paper, wrap well and refrigerate. Then assemble the crêpes up to 3 hours before serving. Swirls of citrus zest make an attractive garnish.

To make the crêpes, in a blender or in a food processor fitted with the metal blade, combine the flour, sugar, salt, egg, egg yolk, 1 cup (8 fl oz/250 ml) of the milk and the melted butter. Process for 30 seconds. Add the remaining ½ cup (4 fl oz/ 125 ml) milk and process until no lumps remain, another 15 seconds. Cover and refrigerate for at least 2 hours or overnight.

In a 6-inch (15-cm) crêpe pan or omelet pan over medium heat, melt 1 tablespoon butter. When it begins to sizzle, swirl to coat the entire surface. Pour off any excess butter. Add a scant ¼ cup (2 fl oz/60 ml) batter to the pan and tilt to coat the bottom and halfway up the sides. Cook for about 90 seconds or until the underside is lightly browned. Flip the crêpe over and cook on the other side for 30 seconds. Transfer to a flat surface. Repeat with the remaining batter, adding more butter as necessary. You should have 8–10 crêpes; trim to make even edges.

To assemble the crêpes, spread 2–3 tablespoons of the preserves in a 4-inch (10-cm) circle in the center of each crêpe. Roll up loosely, or fold in half and then into quarters. In a large sauté pan, warm the 3 tablespoons butter and the amaretto, brandy or orange juice. When simmering, add the crêpes, seam sides down, and sauté, spooning the pan liquid over the tops, until the inside is hot when tested with a small, sharp knife, 4–5 minutes. Transfer to individual plates and spoon on the pan liquid. Sprinkle with the walnuts and serve.

Serves 4

Pear and Honey Clafouti

2 tablespoons unsalted butter, softened, for greasing baking dish, plus 2 tablespoons unsalted butter, melted

4 large pears, about 3 lb (1.5 kg) total weight, peeled, cored and cut into thin slices

1 cup (6 oz/185 g) dried pears, cut into 1-inch (2.5-cm) pieces

1 teaspoon grated lime zest or ½ teaspoon lime oil (see glossary)

4 eggs, lightly beaten

⅓ cup (2½ oz/75 g) firmly packed dark brown sugar

1 cup (8 fl oz/250 ml) half-and-half

⅓ cup (4 oz/125 g) honey

A clafouti is a French dessert of fresh fruit covered with a custard or rich batter and then baked. This version calls for both fresh and dried pears. Use the most flavorful fresh pears you can find; both Royal Riviera and Comice varieties are good choices. Lining the baking pan with aluminum foil makes spills or overflows easy to clean up.

Position a rack in the center of an oven and preheat the oven to 350°F (180°C). Line a baking pan with aluminum foil. Generously grease a 1½-qt (48-fl oz/1.5-l) baking dish or quiche dish with the 2 tablespoons softened butter. Place the dish inside the prepared pan.

Place the fresh pear slices and the dried pears in a bowl. Add the lime zest or lime oil, eggs, brown sugar, the 2 tablespoons melted butter and the half-and-half. Stir gently to mix. Using a spoon, transfer enough of the liquid from the pear mixture to the prepared dish to form a thin layer on the bottom. Using a slotted spoon, transfer the fruit to the dish, arranging it in an even layer atop the cream layer. Then pour the liquid remaining in the bowl evenly over the top. Drizzle the honey evenly over all.

Bake until the top is puffed and golden brown, 25–30 minutes. Serve hot, warm or at room temperature.

Serves 6–8

Apple Fritters

4 Granny Smith or other firm tart
   apples, peeled, cored and sliced into
   ½-inch (12-mm) rings
½ cup (3½ oz/105 g) firmly packed
   light brown sugar
1 cup (5 oz/155 g) all-purpose (plain)
   flour
1 tablespoon vegetable oil, plus oil for
   deep-frying
1 extra-large egg, separated
¾ cup (6 fl oz/180 ml) milk
confectioners' (icing) sugar for topping
maple syrup for topping

*A wonderful brunch dessert, especially when drizzled with dark
amble maple syrup.*

In a bowl, toss together the apple rings and brown sugar
until the apples are evenly coated. Spread on paper towels
to dry slightly.

Sift the flour into a large bowl. Make a well in the center
and add the 1 tablespoon oil and the egg yolk to the well.
While mixing gently with a fork, dribble the milk into the
mixture, stirring to form a smooth batter. In a separate
bowl and using a wire whisk, beat the egg white until it
holds firm peaks. Fold the egg white into the batter.

In a deep frying pan or sauté pan, pour in oil to a depth
of 1½ inches (4 cm) and heat to 375°F (190°C), or until
a bit of the batter turns golden within moments of being
dropped into it. Dip 1 apple ring into the batter and then
allow excess batter to drip back into the bowl. Slip the ring
into the hot oil. Repeat with 1 or 2 more rings. Fry for
4 minutes on one side, then, using a slotted spoon, turn
and fry on the second side for 2–3 minutes. The rings
should be golden brown. Using a slotted spoon, transfer
to paper towels to drain. Repeat with the remaining apple
rings and batter.

Place the warm fritters on a serving platter or on
individual plates. Dust with confectioners' sugar and serve
immediately. Pass the maple syrup.

Serves 4–6

Glossary

The following glossary defines terms specifically as they relate to fruit desserts and their preparation. Included are major and unusual ingredients and basic techniques.

BERRIES

A wide variety of cultivated berries add bright contrasts of color, flavor and texture to fruit desserts. Usually sold in small containers or baskets, they should be checked carefully to make sure that they are firm, plump, and free of blemishes, bruises or mold. Among berry varieties most widely available are:

Blackberries. Juicy, lustrous purple-black berries, at peak of season in summer.

Blueberries. Small, round berries with smooth, dark blue skins, available from late spring through summer. Frozen blueberries, available in food stores year-round, are acceptable substitutes for cooked desserts.

Cranberries. Round, deep red, tart berries, grown primarily in wet, sandy coastal lands—or bogs—in the northeastern United States. Available fresh autumn through early winter and frozen year-round.

Fraises des bois. Tiny wild strawberries, native to France and elsewhere in Europe, prized for their fine, aromatic flavor. Imported and available in specialty-food stores for only a few weeks in late spring or early summer.

Gooseberries. Natives of Europe and very popular in England, these relatives of currants are large, plump round berries (below) with smooth or furry skins in various colors. Green specimens are sharp flavored and best suited to cooking; red ones are sweeter and may be eaten raw. In season early to mid-summer.

Loganberries. These hybrids of the blackberry and raspberry, developed in California and grown throughout the United States, resemble long, shiny raspberries, with a somewhat sharper flavor. Available early to mid-summer.

Raspberries. Sweet, small, red berries with a delicate flavor and tender texture. In peak of season during summer, they are also available frozen year-round for use in cooked desserts.

Strawberries. Probably the most popular berry variety, these plump and juicy, intensely sweet, red, heart-shaped fruits are at their peak from spring into mid-summer.

AMARETTO

Italian liqueur combining essences of apricot and almond.

BRANDY

Applies to any spirit distilled from fermented fruit juice. While the term most specifically refers to dry grape brandy, it also covers dry to sweet distillates of such fruits as apples and berries, whose fruity fragrances lend themselves as flavorings to fruit desserts as well as to after-dinner sipping.

BUTTER, UNSALTED

For the recipes in this book, unsalted butter is preferred. Its light, delicate flavor is better suited to use in desserts than the salted variety.

CALVADOS

Dry French **brandy** distilled from apples and bearing the fruit's distinctive aroma and taste. Dry applejack can be substituted.

CHOCOLATE

To complement fruit desserts, purchase the best-quality chocolate you can find.

Bittersweet Chocolate. Lightly sweetened eating or baking chocolate enriched with extra cocoa butter, which generally accounts for approximately 40 percent of its weight. Look for bittersweet chocolate that contains at least 50 percent cocoa butter.

Semisweet Chocolate. Eating or baking chocolate that is usually—but not always—slightly sweeter than bittersweet chocolate, which can be substituted.

White Chocolate. A chocolatelike product for eating or baking, made by combining pure cocoa butter with sugar, powdered milk and sometimes **vanilla**. Check labels to make sure that the white chocolate you buy is made exclusively with cocoa butter, without the addition of coconut oil or vegetable shortening.

CINNAMON

Popular sweet spice for flavoring baked goods. The aromatic bark of a type of evergreen tree, it is

CHERRIES

Small, round, juicy tree fruits related to the plum, sour to sweet in flavor and with shiny skins ranging from red to orange to purple-black. In season from mid-spring to mid-summer. Select plump, shiny cherries free of blemishes and with their stems attached; avoid any that have split open.

Cherries are easily pitted using a cherry pitter, which holds the fruit and pushes out the pit when pressure is applied. A sharp paring knife can be used as well.

sold as whole dried strips—cinnamon sticks—or ground.

CONDENSED MILK, SWEETENED

A canned product made by evaporating 60 percent of the water from whole milk, then sweetening it with sugar, for use as an ingredient in baked recipes and dessert sauces. Available in the baking section of food stores.

CORNSTARCH

Fine, powdery flour ground from the endosperm of corn—the white heart of the kernel—and used as a neutral-flavored thickening agent in some desserts. Also known as cornflour.

CREAM, HEAVY

Whipping cream with a butterfat content of at least 36 percent. For the best flavor and cooking properties, purchase 100 percent natural fresh cream with a short shelf life printed on the carton; avoid long-lasting varieties that have been processed by ultraheat methods. In Britain, use double cream.

To whip cream, chill it well and place it in a large chilled bowl. With a chilled whisk or electric beaters, beat the cream briskly to the desired consistency, ranging from soft, loose folds to stiff peaks that form when the beaters are lifted out (below). Flavoring or sweetener can be added before or during whipping.

CREAM OF TARTAR

Acidic powder extracted during wine making that is used as an additive to meringue, serving both to stabilize the egg whites and to increase their heat tolerance. Also used as a leavening agent, most commonly combined with baking soda to make commercial baking powder, and as an ingredient in sugar syrups to prevent crystallization.

CRÈME DE CASSIS

Sweet, red liqueur made by steeping black currants in grape brandy.

CRÈME FRAÎCHE

French-style lightly soured and thickened fresh cream, generally used as a topping or garnish for sweet or savory dishes. Increasingly available in food markets, although a similar product can be prepared at home by stirring 2 teaspoons well-drained sour cream into 1 cup (8 fl oz/250 ml) lightly whipped **heavy** (double) **cream**. Or, to make your own crème fraîche, stir 1 teaspoon cultured buttermilk into 1 cup (8 fl oz/250 ml) heavy (double) cream. Cover tightly and leave at warm room temperature until thickened, about 12 hours. Refrigerate until ready to serve. Will keep for up to 1 week.

FIGS

Late-summer and early-autumn fruits characterized by their many tiny edible seeds, sweet, slightly astringent flavor and soft, succulent texture. It is best to buy fresh figs ripe and use them immediately.

FILO

Tissue-thin sheets of flour-and-water pastry used throughout the Middle East as crisp wrappers for sweet or savory fillings. Usually found in the frozen-food section of well-stocked food stores, or can be purchased fresh in Middle Eastern delicatessens; defrost frozen filo thoroughly before use. The fragile sheets, which generally measure 10 by 14 inches (25 by 35 cm), must be separated and handled carefully to avoid tearing. As you work with the filo, keep the sheets covered to prevent them from drying out. The name derives from the Greek word for leaf.

FLOUR, ALL-PURPOSE

The most common flour for baking, this bleached and blended (hard and soft wheats) variety is

EGGS

Eggs are sold in food stores in a range of sizes; the most common U.S. standards are jumbo, extra large, large and medium.

Separating Eggs

To separate an egg, crack the shell in half by tapping it against the side of a bowl and then breaking it apart with your fingers. Holding the shell halves over the bowl, gently transfer the whole yolk back and forth between them, letting the clear white drop away into the bowl. Take care not to cut into the yolk with the edges of the shell (the whites will not beat properly if they contain any yolk). Transfer the yolk to another bowl.

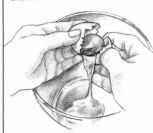

The same basic function is also performed by an aluminum, ceramic or plastic egg separator placed over a bowl. The separator holds the yolk intact in its cuplike center while allowing the white to drip out through one or more slots in its side into the bowl.

available in all food markets. Also called plain flour.

FLOUR, CAKE

Very fine-textured bleached flour for use in cakes and other baked goods. Also called soft-wheat flour. **All-purpose** (plain) **flour** is not an acceptable substitute.

GELATIN

Unflavored commercial gelatin gives delicate body to mousses and molded desserts. Sold in envelopes holding about 1 tablespoon (¼ oz/7 g), each of which is sufficient to jell about 2 cups (16 fl oz/500 ml) liquid.

GRAND MARNIER

A popular commercial brand of orange-flavored liqueur, distinguished by its pure Cognac base.

HALF-AND-HALF

A commercial dairy product consisting of half milk and half light cream. In Britain known as half cream.

KIRSCH

Dry, clear **brandy** distilled from black morello cherries and infused with their unique aroma and taste. Do not confuse with crème de kirsch, a sweet cherry liqueur.

KIWIFRUITS

Also known as the Chinese gooseberry, after its country of origin, these fruits are noteworthy for their fuzzy brown skins concealing sweet, juicy, bright green flesh with flavor reminiscent of melon and berries. The fruit yields gently to the touch when ripe. Buy them ripe if to be used immediately, or firm, allowing them to ripen in the refrigerator for a few days.

LEMON OIL
Aromatic oil cold-pressed from the **zest** of lemons, used sparingly as a flavoring in baked goods and desserts. Available at specialty-food stores.

LIME OIL
Aromatic oil cold-pressed from the **zest** of tropical limes, used sparingly as a flavoring in baked goods and desserts. Available at specialty-food stores.

MANGO
Tropical fruits with juicy, aromatic orange flesh. Ripe mangoes yield slightly to finger pressure; ripen firm mangoes at room temperature in an open paper or plastic bag. Slit with a knife, the skin peels easily. Slice the flesh from both sides of the large, flat pit, as well as from around its edges.

MARGARINE
Solid form of vegetable fat processed to resemble the taste, texture and appearance of butter. Although its flavor cannot compare to butter's full richness, margarine can be used as a substitute by those who wish to limit animal fats in their diet.

MASCARPONE CHEESE
A thick Italian cream cheese, usually sold in tubs and similar to French **crème fraîche.** Look for mascarpone in the cheese case of an Italian delicatessen or a specialty-food shop.

OATS, ROLLED
Flakes of oat that have been flattened by passing them through heated rollers after they have been cleaned and hulled. A popular and widely available form of the cereal, for use in baked goods and to lend a rich, crunchy topping to desserts.

ORANGE, NAVEL
Seedless, sweet, easily peeled orange, recognizable for the navel-like indentation at its flower end.

PAPAYA
Tropical fruit shaped somewhat like a large **pear** or avocado, with soft, sweet orange flesh—milder tasting than a **mango**—and smooth yellow skin. When ripe, a papaya yields gently to finger pressure; ripen green papayas in a bowl at room temperature. Halve lengthwise and scoop out the shiny black seeds before peeling.

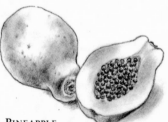

PINEAPPLE
These most popular of tropical fruits, with their distinctive pinecone shapes—the source of their name—should always be purchased in the fully ripe form. To test, smell the fruit, which should have a distinctively sweet aroma; you should also be able to easily pull out a top, center leaf from a fully ripe fruit.

PEARS
Subtly sweet and aromatic, and smooth to grainy in texture, pears of many varieties are a favorite fruit for eating or cooking year-round. Anjou pears, available from autumn through mid-spring, are rich in flavor, with a hint of spice and a smooth texture; among the largest and plumpest of pears, they have short necks and thin, yellow-green skins. Bartlett pears, also called Williams' pears, are medium-sized and shaped roughly like bells, with creamy yellow skins sometimes tinged in red; fine-textured, juicy and mild tasting, they are equally good for cooking or eating and are available from summer to early autumn. Comice pears, available from autumn through early winter, are sweet and juicy; large, round and short-necked, they have greenish yellow skins tinged with red. Royal Riviera pears, available in winter and favored for eating or cooking, are among the most luxurious of all—large, with red-tinged skins and juicy, smooth, sweet flesh.

Royal Riviera

Comice

POMEGRANATE
Autumn fruit of Persian origin, shaped like a large orange, with leathery red skin concealing hundreds of bright ruby-red seeds about the size and shape of small corn kernels. The seeds are composed largely of a juicy, sweet pulp, and can be eaten on their own, used as colorful garnishes, or squeezed to yield a juice that becomes a sweet, aromatic flavoring in its own right.

PORT
Sweet, robust fortified wine from Portugal. Sipped on its own usually at the end of the meal, port can also be used to flavor fruit desserts or sauces.

PUFF PASTRY
Form of pastry in which pastry dough and butter or some other solid fat are repeatedly layered to form thin leaves that puff up to flaky lightness when baked.

RHUBARB
Perennial plant whose stems resemble large, salmon-colored celery stalks. Although technically a vegetable, rhubarb is most commonly eaten as a fruit, cooked and sweetened with sugar and often combined with strawberries or raspberries. Avoid the leaves and roots, which can be toxic.

RUM
Any of a wide variety of spirits distilled from sugarcane or molasses, a specialty of the Caribbean. So-called light or white rums are clear, fairly flavorless spirits; dark or Demerara rums carry some of the caramel color and distinctive flavor of their sources.

SHERRY

Fortified, cask-aged wine, ranging from dry to sweet; enjoyed as an aperitif and used as a flavoring in both savory and sweet recipes.

SUGARS

Many different forms of sugar may be used to sweeten fruit desserts.

Brown Sugar. A rich-tasting granulated sugar combined with molasses in varying quantities to yield golden, light or dark brown sugar, with crystals varying from coarse to finely granulated. Widely available in the baking section of food stores.

Confectioners' Sugar. Finely pulverized sugar, also known as powdered or icing sugar, which dissolves quickly and provides a thin, white decorative coating. To prevent confectioners' sugar from absorbing moisture in the air and caking, manufacturers often mix a little **cornstarch** into it.

Granulated Sugar. The standard, widely used form of pure white sugar. Do not use superfine granulated sugar unless specified.

Superfine Sugar. Granulated sugar ground to form extra-fine granules that dissolve quickly in liquids and are ideal for some baking recipes. In Britain use caster sugar.

Coarse Sugar. Coarsely granulated sugar used to decorate a wide range of desserts.

TAPIOCA, INSTANT

Finely ground flakes of the tropical manioc plant's dried, starchy root. Used as a thickener in pies, tarts and puddings.

VANILLA EXTRACT

Flavoring derived by dissolving the essential oil of the vanilla bean in an alcohol base. Use only products labeled "pure" or "natural" vanilla extract (essence).

STONE FRUITS

Plump and juicy, many different kinds of stone fruits—tree fruits containing single large, hard pits, or "stones," at their centers—make excellent main ingredients in fresh or cooked fruit desserts from late spring into early autumn.

Apricots
Early-ripening summer fruits, natives of China but now grown throughout the world. Buy fairly firm, blemish-free apricots, avoiding any tinged with green. Complete ripening at room temperature until soft.

Nectarines
Smooth-skinned, slightly smaller relatives of the peach, these juicy fruits have a rich, slightly spicy flavor. Select firm, unblemished specimens without any hint of green. Ripen at room temperature, then keep in the refrigerator for up to a week.

Peaches
With slightly fuzzy skins ranging from creamy yellow to deep gold and red, and flesh ranging from pale yellow to deep orange, peaches are plump, sweet and intensely juicy fruits.

Plums
More than a thousand different varieties exist of this smooth, shiny-skinned, sweet-tart fruit, ranging from green and red to the deep blue-black of Italian plums—the variety dried to make prunes. Purchase firm, plump fruits free of blemishes.

To Pit Stone Fruits

For easy removal of the pits from stone fruits, try to buy varieties—particularly of peaches and plums—designated "freestone," indicating stones that separate easily.

With a small, sharp knife, carefully cut the fruit in half down to the pit, through the stem end and following the slight indentation or ridge along one side of the fruit.

Grasp the two halves of the cut fruit with your hands and twist, pulling them apart.

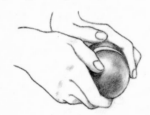

Pull out the pit from the half within which it remains. If it clings to the fruit, use a knife to carefully pry or cut it out.

YEAST, ACTIVE DRY

One of the most widely available forms of yeast for baking, commonly sold in individual packages containing a scant 1 tablespoon (¼ oz/7 g) and found in the baking section of food stores. Seek out one of the new strains of quick-rise yeast available in specialty-food stores. If using fresh cake yeast, substitute ½ oz (15 g) for 1 tablespoon active dry yeast.

ZEST

Thin, brightly colored, outermost layer of a citrus fruit's peel, containing most of its aromatic essential oils—a lively source of flavor in fruit desserts. Zest may be removed using one of two easy methods:

1. Use a simple tool known as a zester, drawing its sharp-edged holes across the fruit's skin to remove the zest in thin strips. Alternatively, use a fine hand-held grater.

2. Holding the edge of a paring knife or vegetable peeler away from you and almost parallel to the fruit's skin, carefully cut off the zest in thin strips, taking care not to remove any white pith with it. Then thinly slice or chop on a cutting board.

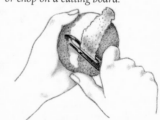

Index

ACKNOWLEDGMENTS

The publishers would like to thank the following people and organizations for their generous assistance and support in producing this book:
Sharon C. Lott, Stephen W. Griswold, Ken DellaPenta, Jennifer Mullins, Jennifer Hauser, Tarji Mickelson, the buyers for Gardener's Eden,
and the buyers and store managers for Hold Everything, Pottery Barn and Williams-Sonoma stores.

The following kindly lent props for the photography:
Biordi Art Imports, Candelier, Fillamento, Fredericksen Hardware, J. Goldsmith Antiques,
Sue Fisher King, Lorraine Puckett, RH, and Chuck Williams.